How to Buy (and Survive!) Your First Computer

Carolee Nance Kolve

McGraw-Hill Book Company

New York St. Louis San Francisco Auckland
Bogotá Hamburg Johannesburg London Madrid
Mexico Montreal New Delhi Panama Paris
São Paulo Singapore Sydney Tokyo Toronto

Library of Congress Cataloging in Publication Data

Kolve, Carolee Nance.
  How to buy (and survive!) your first computer.

  Includes index.
    1. Small business—Data processing.   2. Electronic
digital computers.   I. Title.
HF5548.2.K596   1983   001.64′068′7   83-795
ISBN 0-07-035130-9

1234567890   BKPBKP   898765432

ISBN 0-07-035130-9

The editors for this book were Stephen G. Guty and Virginia Fechtmann Blair,
the designer was Jules Perlmutter, and the production
supervisor was Sally Fliess. It was set in Korinna
by University Graphics, Inc.
Printed and bound by The Book Press.

Sadly, the English language does not have a general pronoun which
can be conveniently substituted for he or she. As any writer
will acknowledge, it is terribly cumbersome to write he or she,
him or her, businessperson, and so on in every sentence. So I
have taken a stand and used he, him, and
businessman. You see, I know that women in the business
community are broad-minded enough to forgive me and I wasn't
sure about you men!

To my husband, Jerry,
who encouraged me, bragged about me, and
was the first to read this book,
but who still thinks
his business doesn't need a computer.

And to our son, Kristopher,
to whom the Computer Age belongs.
At three months, he has his parents
perfectly programmed.

And to my beloved grandfather,
the late Paul H. (Tex) Talbert, who
inspired me in all ways,
always.

About the Author

Carolee Kolve has spent 15 years in the computer industry in a variety of technical, marketing, and management positions—all dealing with the first-time computer user. She understands the fears, concerns, and real problems which arise when a small business acquires its first computer.

A graduate of Stanford University, Carolee began her data processing career with the IBM Corporation. In 12 years with IBM, she earned 9 promotions and a reputation as a top marketing manager. Her sales team was ranked number one in the United States in the sale of small business computers and she received numerous awards and honors. She then spent 2 years as director of marketing for a highly innovative marketing company that sold several major brand computers to small businesses. This experience gave her wide exposure to the numerous computer products on the market today and the problems facing a business executive in trying to make a selection. Today, Carolee is an independent computer consultant, with clients in Los Angeles, San Francisco, and Portland. She helps the small businessman determine if he is ready for a computer and advises him in all aspects of computer evaluation, cost justification, and selection. She has taught principles of data processing to over 2000 business executives throughout the United States, Europe, and the Far East.

Carolee lives in Portland, Oregon, with her husband Jerry, President of Kolve Sawchain Company, and their infant son, Kristopher.

Contents

Preface

We are all aware of the increasing computerization of our world. Whether we are prepared for them or not, computers are here—sending man to the moon and most of our mail to us. Because of the incredible technological break-throughs of the past decade, computers are now decidedly affordable. Marketing studies indicate that one and a half million small businesses will acquire their first computer during the next three years, and literally hundreds of computer companies are springing up to fill this need.

The chief obstacles standing between the typical small business and its first computer are confusion and fear. An executive may wonder: Am I ready for a computer? How do I choose among the hundreds available? How will it affect my people and my customers? How do I prevent some of the horror stories I've heard about? How do I know I'm getting the right software? And what is software anyway??? Literally hundreds of questions regarding computers pop into the executive's mind and cause enough uncertainty that many executives choose to do nothing.

The owner of a small business knows his company inside and out. He understands production and finance and marketing and can comfortably make decisions in these arenas. But today's executive has had little direct exposure to computers and his decision-making confidence level is simply too low. The first purpose of this book, therefore, is to raise that level by giving you the knowledge and confidence you need to make a sound evalu-ation of your readiness for a computer.

This is not a technical book. It is not intended to make you a computer expert or "snow" you with irrelevant technical details. It will address those questions about computers which are important to an executive trying to decide whether or not to get one:

- Are you ready for a computer?
- Approximately how much will you have to spend?

- What are the important facts about hardware and software that an executive needs to know?
- What benefits can you expect to achieve?
- How are computers cost-justified?

The second purpose of this book is to help you select a computer vendor without having to pay a $5,000 to $15,000 consulting fee. Every computer salesman on earth knows his product is the right one for you. This book will arm you for the barrage of salesmanship you are going to encounter when you let the first one know you might be looking. And it will enable you to exercise those salesmen just as a consultant would to be sure you are getting all the facts you need.

Questions covered include:

- How do you evaluate software to be sure it fits your needs?
- How much computer horsepower do you need for today and tomorrow?
- What criteria should you use in comparing computer vendors?
- What support services should you have to ensure success?
- How can you negotiate the best possible purchase?
- How do you protect yourself with a contract that makes sure your business won't become a computer disaster?

The third purpose of this book is to help you establish realistic expectations for the computer. There exists, in fact, a certain conspiratorial silence among computer sales people. Very few will ever tell you up front how much effort the computer will require, how long it will take to get it up and running and how much it will end up costing. They are afraid you would never buy one if you knew. And they're afraid that if they give you the bad news, another salesman will come along, paint a rosier picture, and win the sale. My favorite client once told me that buying a computer was like having a child. If he had known in advance the hassle and expense involved, he would never have done it, but he's glad he didn't know because now he would never get rid of it! This book will alert you to some of the pitfalls that exist and what some very successful computer users have done to avoid them.

Lastly, let me tell you that I am a tremendous fan of computers and what they can do for a small business. They are perhaps the most significant management productivity tool of our lifetime and I believe your business will become increasingly hampered without one. To put it more positively, the increased control you will have over your business will help you grow profitably and save you hours of frustration and tedium. Your employees will be more productive and find their morale improving as new skills are learned and boring tasks are eliminated. Used creatively, a computer will help you, the executive, more than anyone in the company. But first, you have to understand it.

HOW TO USE THIS BOOK

I have written this book assuming that the reader has had no prior exposure to computers. Obviously for some of you, this is not the case. Depending on your knowledge level and your needs, here is what to read:

If you have had no prior exposure to computers and want to see if one might suit your business, read Part I.

If you have taken one or more computer seminars, but are not sure if your business is ready for a computer, read Chapters 1, 3, 4, 5, 7, and 8.

If you are convinced you need a computer and are ready to select one, read Part II.

If you have bought a computer, read Part III and Chapters 3 and 8.

The book contains educational information (text) as well as worksheets for determining if a computer can be cost-justified, deciding which size computer your business will need, evaluating vendors, and so on. If you are reading simply for an understanding of the issues involved with getting a computer, ignore the worksheets and go back to them later.

ACKNOWLEDGMENTS

Everything valuable that we learn in the computer business, we learn through experience. For those experiences which have helped me both through the years and in the writing of this book, I wish to thank

Some special clients and customers:

Jim Bushman of Snowden Penser
Pat and Luella Connelly of Creative Teaching Press
Grant Dean of Dean Distributing
Tom Platner of Santa Cruz County
Floyd Runyan of Cashco
Bill Schultz of Southern California Marine Association
Bob Smith of Republic Electronic Supply
Chuck Tauman of Willner, Bennett, Bobbitt & Hartman
Jim Truesdell of Kingsley Manufacturing
Wendell Walker of Scotsco

and some favorite bosses, colleagues, employees, and friends:

Susan and Bob Adams   Tom Jenkins
Jack Andersen   John Johnson
Dave Baum   Marlene Mallicoat
Marvi Bennion Briscoe   Dave Merrill
Dave Carlson   Harvey Rich
Dirk Eastman   Gary Smith
Ernie Fraser   Gayle Strickland
Gary Gibson   Ken Virnig
Bob Hardy

for their extra assistance in the writing of this book, I thank Sue Nance, my lovely mother, for her help in everything and particularly for her relentless perusal of my spelling and grammar,

Dick Vink, computer consultant and friend, for his expert advice and editing; and

Beth Peetz, my extraordinary word processing specialist, who typed and retyped this to perfection.

Finally, for their lifelong support and encouragement, I wish to thank my grandparents Tex and Dorothy Talbert and my parents, Sue and Forrest Nance.

What to Consider before Buying a Computer

Are You Ready for a Computer?

Until recently, a business needed to be of substantial size to justify buying a computer. Computer salesmen looked for businesses with annual sales of at least $2 million and 3 or more clerks in the office. Today, offices with 1 or 2 clerks and far less than $1 million in sales are finding that a computer is affordable. Being ready for a computer is therefore more a case of wanting one than an issue of affordability. After all, a minicomputer, financed over 3 to 5 years, costs far less than hiring an additional person. A microcomputer suitable for business is only a few hundred dollars a month when financed over 1 year! Whether you have a one-person law firm or medical practice or are a small manufacturer, contractor, or distributor, there is a computer you can afford.

WHY BUY A COMPUTER?

What motivates the business executive to begin the search for the right computer? Why does he or she suddenly feel ready? Many are motivated by business concerns—the nagging feeling that things aren't quite as simple as they used to be. The business or professional practice has grown and they find it more difficult to stay on top of their key assets: Accounts Receivable and Inventory. They are concerned about the rising number of stockouts as well as the rising cost of carrying inventory. Employee morale is low and turnover is too high. They don't have the necessary information to determine which areas of the business are profitable and which are not. They believe a computer might be the solution.

Many other executives develop their interest in computers when business is going quite well. Perhaps they are contemplating rapid business growth and realize that a computer will help manage that growth effectively and at the same time control the overhead. Perhaps a friendly customer, competitor, or business associate has just gotten a computer and raves about the results. Or a son, daughter, or employee has recently taken a computer course and is making encouraging remarks. Many people are simply intrigued by technology. Whatever the reason, most executives experience increasing interest and just *know* when they are ready to look. If you are beginning to have that inkling, you are not alone. During the eighties, almost every business will acquire some type of computer.

The biggest obstacles to taking the plunge, however, are the concerns and fears mentioned in the Preface. Fears that a computer will disrupt the business, be a negative factor with employees or customers, and cost more than anticipated can abort the decision to acquire one. Many small businessmen today are caught between interest in computerizing their companies and reluctance to take a risk. If you are in this in-between state, the following checklist may help. The more yes answers you have, the more likely it is that you are indeed ready for automation.

ARE YOU READY CHECKLIST

- ☐ Is your business healthy and growing?
- ☐ If you are experiencing a business slump, is it due to seasonality or predictably temporary conditions?
- ☐ Is your staff putting in much overtime?
- ☐ Can you foresee adding an additional clerk during the next 12 months?
- ☐ Is morale high in your office? Is there team spirit and interest in the business?
- ☐ If morale is not what you would like, could it be due to tedium and overwork?
- ☐ Is your Accounts Receivable growing disproportionately to revenue?
- ☐ Do you find some of your "best" customers, clients, or patients not paying as quickly as they used to?
- ☐ Is cash flow or workload so tight that you are occasionally missing Accounts Payable discounts?
- ☐ Are stockouts disrupting your customer service and causing you to lose profitable sales?
- ☐ Do you have finished goods which cannot be shipped for lack of parts?
- ☐ Does your inventory investment sneak up higher than you'd like and sometimes with the wrong items?

☐ Do you spend more time on paperwork than you used to?

☐ Do you hear more customer complaints than you used to?

☐ Does it take longer to fill an order than it used to?

☐ Do you have a hunch that some salesmen aren't selling the full product line or using their time as productively as your best reps?

☐ Do you ever wish that you could get information about sales or profitability that no one has time to put together for you?

☐ Are some of your competitors now using computers?

☐ Do you feel that you don't have as much time for customers, for planning, or for golf as you'd like?

☐ Do you have an employee, son, daughter, or spouse who has expressed an interest in computers?

☐ Can you take the time to get involved in the selection of the computer and in setting the objectives and requirements for its performance?

☐ Is it a priority to you that your business be on the leading edge competitively?

☐ Are you looking for ways to increase productivity and profitability?

☐ Do you have solid confidence in your ability to manage and lead your people?

☐ Does the idea of working harder than usual for a short period of time stimulate you rather than turn you off?

If you answered yes to at least ten of these questions, you probably know you are a serious candidate for a computer. If you answered yes to the last five questions, you can feel confident that your computer installation would be a success.

2

What Do You Need to Know About Computers?

As you begin to talk to computer people, you will be inundated with their terminology. Some of the technical aspects of a computer will be important to you. Others will not. This chapter will review certain computer terms, principles, and functions which a business executive needs to know. If you have already taken a computer seminar and are familiar with the following terms and concepts, you may want to skip this chapter.

COMPUTER CONCEPTS CHECKLIST:

☐ Input
☐ Storage
☐ Process
☐ Output
☐ CRT, tube, screen, display, terminal
☐ Winchester disk, megabyte, removable, fixed
☐ Diskette, floppy disk
☐ Magnetic tape
☐ Backup
☐ CPU, memory, chip
☐ Letter-quality printer, dot-matrix printer, line printer
☐ File, record, field

☐ Master file, index
☐ Transaction file
☐ Updating
☐ Sorting
☐ Reference reports
☐ Exception reports
☐ Ranking reports
☐ Inquiries

THE PRINCIPLE OF DATA PROCESSING

The most significant principle of a computer is that you, as a human, need to handle information only *once.* Then, you sit back and let the computer use it and reuse it. For example, you tell the computer an employee's pay rate and the number of hours he worked and the computer produces a payroll check, a union report, 941s, W-2s, department and company reports, and so on. The computer eliminates the repetitive and mundane handling of information. It can sort, sift, select, and summarize information so that you see what you need when you need it.

HOW DOES A COMPUTER WORK?

Surprisingly, a computer processes information or "data" much as you do. Contrary to its image as an enormously complex creation of brilliant (if not slightly weird) minds, the computer is really a very logical and straightforward tool, which will do precisely what you tell it. Its processing capabilities and functions are not all that different from yours, just faster.

The four functional elements of a computer include:

1. Input
2. Storage
3. Processing
4. Output

If someone asked you to multiply six times seven and give the answer, you would be using these same four functions. Your eyes or ears allow you to receive the input (6 × 7), your brain has stored the multiplication tables and performs (processes) the arithmetic, and your mouth supplies the output when you say 42. A computer is composed of specialized equipment which is built to perform these four functions. To give you an idea of the difference in speed between people and computers, a fast computer could have done this calculation about 15 billion times while you read the problem!

There are hundreds of computers on the market today, ranging from economical personal computers, or microcomputers, to the more expensive minicomputers, superminis, and mainframes. All of them have the same functional elements.

Input

Computers receive your instructions and information through a variety of means. The most common today is a work station made up of a cathode ray tube, or television screen, and a keyboard. (This is referred to as a "CRT," or a "screen," a "display," a "video display terminal," a "VDT," a "terminal," or a "tube.") It looks just like a TV with a typewriter keyboard attached. Information that you type for the computer is displayed in front of you so you can conveniently make corrections. Then everything you have typed is sent to the computer to be stored or processed.

You may also have seen punched cards. Some of the bills you receive are prepared on cards which are punched with your account number and the amount you owe. As these are returned with your payment, they are automatically read by a computer input device called a card reader. Thus the computer knows you have paid and no clerical time has been expended.

Storage

Information that you enter into the computer needs to be retained so that it can be used again. For example, you can type into the computer all your customer names and addresses. You do this once and then they are stored permanently so they can be automatically printed on invoices, statements, labels, shipping documents, reports, and so on.

Disks

The most common storage medium on any type of computer is called a "disk." It is a circular metal platter resembling a phonograph record and information is recorded on it in concentric tracks. The disk is housed in a disk "drive" which is attached to the computer and contains the mechanism which reads and writes on the disk. The storage capacity of a disk is measured in "bytes." Each byte will hold one character, either a letter or a number. There are two types of disks: (1) large metal disks, commonly called "hard disks"; and (2) smaller, flexible disks called "floppy disks" or "diskettes."

Personal computers generally use the diskettes. The storage capacity of a diskette is usually measured in thousands of bytes. Depending on size, diskettes will hold from 80,000 to over 1 million characters. Depending on how much data you need to store, one, two, or more diskette drives, each holding one diskette, may be attached to a personal computer.

For businesses needing more storage, hard disks are available in many sizes—from 5 million bytes (expressed as 5 megabytes) up to over 200 megabytes. To put this in perspective, if your customer names and addresses took 100 bytes (letters and numbers) each, a 5-megabyte disk would hold 50,000 customers.

Most personal computers (microcomputers) use either diskettes or the smaller hard disks, typically 5 megabytes. Minicomputers always have a hard disk.

Floppy versus Hard Disks:

Microcomputers using diskettes (floppy disks) as the only storage medium are less expensive than those with a hard disk. They also, of course, have less "on-line" storage capacity (information available to the computer at any one time). Some businesses buy them thinking that they will keep Accounts Payable on one diskette, Mailing Lists on another, and so on. (The diskettes are only $3.00 to $10.00 each.) Then, depending on what they are doing, they will give the computer the appropriate diskette. This works, but many companies find it confusing to keep changing diskettes. If an employee wants to ask the computer a question about a customer account while the customer is on the phone, he may have to stop what he is doing and find the right diskette.

It is definitely more convenient to have all the information about your business on-line all of the time. Of course, if all your information fits on one diskette, then a floppy system may be fine. Hard disks not only hold more, but they are five to ten times faster. Almost everything you do on your computer involves reading or writing on the disk, so speed can be very significant. Many businesses start with diskettes and later add a hard disk to improve their computer response time.

If you have more than one CRT, or work station, on your computer, you will clearly need a hard disk for speed. There are two types of hard disks on the market: (1) "Winchester disks," which are sealed inside the computer; and (2) "removable disks," which are inside a cartridge and can be taken in and out of the computer. Each of these types of disks may range in size from 5 to 50 megabytes. Of the two, the Winchester is the newer, more reliable piece of technology. It is the only type of hard disk found in microcomputers. Because the disk is sealed inside the computer, it is protected from the environment. Also, the mechanism which records and reads the disk is built to work with the disk without scratching or damaging it. The removable disk cartridge (available only on some minicomputers) does not have these advantages, is more prone to mechanical difficulties, and usually costs more. Its advantage, however, is extended storage capacity, that is, if you don't mind changing disk cartridges. Since the Winchester is permanently in the computer, you can't take it out and put in another disk containing additional information. You can, however, do this with removable disk packs. (You could have one pack for Payroll, one for Inventory, and so on.) But most businesses find that it is easiest to keep all their information on-line simultaneously, so they usually buy a Winchester which is large enough to hold all their data.

Backup

Contrary to the disaster stories you may have heard, today's computers rarely "go haywire" and destroy your business records. It is possible, however, to erase a disk, post payments twice, or destroy the data you have stored. To eliminate the damage which could result, all data should be "backed up" daily. This simply means making a copy of your business records at the end of each day. Then, if a problem arises tomorrow, you go back to today's records and enter only the intervening transactions. Without backup, you would have to start from scratch. If you have a Winchester disk system, you will also have either a diskette drive or magnetic tape unit to use for backup.

Magnetic Tape

As was just mentioned, magnetic tape is another medium for storage. It is available in cartridge or reel, just as you might use on a tape recorder. Tape is very useful for backup but is too limiting to use as primary storage. Tape has to be read in sequence from start to finish, whereas a disk can be read randomly. In other words, with your customers on disk, you can ask the computer for a particular customer's balance and get the answer immediately. If your customers are on tape, you have to wait for the whole reel to be read until you find the customer. For backing up a large Winchester disk, a tape cartridge is a quick and easy device, although it is more expensive than a diskette. If you have 20 megabytes or more to be backed up, using diskettes could take a half hour or more because you are feeding many diskettes in to be copied, one at a time. A tape cartridge holds more than a diskette and you can put it in, start the backup and leave.

Processing

Processing is the term used to describe the main activity of the computer. The device which does the processing is the heart and brain of the computer and is called, not surprisingly, the "central processing unit" (CPU).

What is computer processing? The primary capabilities of the CPU are arithmetic, logic, and control of input and output activities. If you input a string of numbers to be accumulated, it is the CPU which gets the numbers and does the addition. If you input the details of a customer order, it is the CPU which computes the amount owed to you. If you ask the computer for a list of customers who are over their credit limit, the CPU uses a logic capability to identify the culprits. It actually reviews each customer stored on the disk and compares what he owes to his credit limit. If the balance due is greater than the credit limit, the customer is selected for printing. The entire process of reading, comparing, and selecting is performed by the CPU and is called "processing."

Without processing, computers would have no value. Every computer, from the smallest, costing $1,000, to the largest, costing over $1,000,000 has a CPU. All CPUs have the same function and capabilities: the ability to receive input, to act upon it, and to output the results. The more sophisticated and expensive CPUs are larger, they perform at faster speeds, and they are capable of performing multiple tasks at once. The capability of the CPU is determined by the amount of memory available to it and its internal speed.

The term memory is somewhat misleading because the permanent storage place is the disk. The disk permanently stores all the information about your business: customer names, addresses, terms, accounts receivable figures, sales history, and so on. The CPU memory is temporary, transitional—more like a passing thought than what you might think of as memory. The CPU uses its memory to solve problems or process information and it's all over in a flash.

For example, if you are using the computer to do Payroll, you will input the number of hours each employee worked. The CPU takes your input (hours), finds the employee's hourly rate on the disk where it is permanently stored (until he gets a raise), and multiplies the two. The gross pay is then put on the disk where it can be picked up when it's time to print checks. At this point, the hours, rate, and gross pay are erased from the CPU memory as it goes on to process the next employee. The CPU memory is very much like a temporary scratch pad. It is only concerned with the job at hand.

Because CPU memory is temporary, it needs to hold only the instructions (multiply rate times hours) and the data currently being processed (e.g., $5.00, 40 hours). The disk, on the other hand, needs to hold every employee's rate, hours, and name as well as all your customer and inventory information. Thus CPU size is generally measured in thousands of characters, or positions of storage, while disk size is measured in millions.

Small business computers most commonly have CPUs with 64,000 positions of memory. This is called a "64K CPU" (K standing for Kilo or 1,000). This size memory will accommodate most of the typical business applications you may choose to put on your computer: Order Processing, Inventory Control, Accounts Receivable, Sales Analysis, Payroll, Accounts Payable, and General Ledger as well as Word Processing. Financial modeling applications which use a lot of information at once may require additional memory.

The memory required relates directly to the size and complexity of the job to be done. Some of the small microcomputers have application packages which run in only 48K, while some minicomputers have highly sophisticated programs which require 128K or more.

If the volume of work that you do is such that you need more than one input screen, you may also need more memory. If you have two people working with the computer simultaneously, they both need to use the CPU memory for their instructions (program) and input data. Sometimes, a 64K CPU can handle two or more concurrent users—it depends largely on the complexity of programs being used. (Programs will be discussed more extensively in the chapter on software.)

When describing computers, the salesman may refer to two types of CPU memory: ROM and RAM. ROM stands for "read only memory" and it is essentially invisible to you. It is preprogrammed by the computer manufacturer to cause the computer to perform certain functions. You can do nothing to change it or erase it. RAM stands for "random access memory" and this is the memory which is used for your programs. When you are comparing the capability of two computers, it is RAM which you normally discuss. (RAM is essentially synonymous with the CPU memory just mentioned.)

In addition to being distinguished by size, CPUs are sometimes distinguished by the type of internal processor "chip" they use. There are a handful of electronics firms which make the technical "innards" for virtually all the hundreds of computers on the market. Insiders in the industry will follow closely which chip is used in each computer, but the brand type is not of great significance to the end user. You should know, however, that chips are distinguished according to processing capability and that in small business computers, there are two major kinds: "8-bit" and "16-bit." These terms are defined in the glossary, but the significance to you is that a 16-bit machine costs more, is faster, and has more growth capacity. If your business grows and you need to add more input screens, a 16-bit machine will carry you further because you can add the additional CPU memory needed to accommodate many simultaneous computer users.

Output

After the computer computes, or processes your data, you need to see the results. Information is communicated to you through an output device. One kind of output device is the same CRT used for input. You can walk up to a CRT and type in a customer's name; the CPU will find the customer's balance due and sales year-to-date and output this information back to you on the display screen. Another type of output device is the same disk used for storage. As invoices are computed and printed, the CPU can automatically update the customer Accounts Receivable and Inventory information on the disk.

Printers

Most computer output is printed: invoices, payroll checks, sales reports, and so on; so the most common output device is, of course, the printer. Printers come in several "flavors": "letter-quality" printers, "dot-matrix" printers, and "line" printers.

Letter-quality printers are best if you plan to use your computer extensively to produce letters or mailing labels which go to the public. They are relatively slow (usually printing from 12 to 80 characters per second) and more expensive than other printers of comparable speed. The quality of the print is superb and it is impossible to distinguish from typewriter copy, because the printed characters are fully formed by the same type of mechanism found on a typewriter: selectric type ball, daisy wheel, or thimble.

If most of your printing is for internal company use, the expense of the letter-quality printer is unnecessary. A dot-matrix printer is the most reasonable in price. These printers create characters from individual dots as the print mechanism moves across the page. Small wires strike a ribbon to form the dots for each character. Speeds range from 35 to 180 characters per second. Good quality matrix printers print the dots close together so the letters look *almost* typed. This is called "correspondence quality," not quite *letter* quality, but very good.

Some microcomputers can be hooked up to reconditioned typewriters, thus becoming low-cost, letter-quality printers. Unfortunately, typewriters were not built to be driven by a computer and the reliability is poor.

The fastest printers are line printers, which produce an entire line of characters at once using a whirling print chain. These will operate at speeds from 100 to 1200 lines per minute. Some laser printers on the market will print 18,000 lines per minute. This is so fast, it's hard to relate to. But a "slow" 100-line-per-minute printer goes at the speed of twenty top-notch typists. The laser printer could keep up with 3,600 typists! Because of their cost, line printers are normally found only on minicomputers or on computers larger than minicomputers.

IMPORTANT COMPUTER CAPABILITIES

The discussion of computer devices or "hardware" is a bit dry, but important. Before you begin relating this to your business, you need to understand one more technical concept.

The heart of the computer is its processing, or computing, capability. However, of equal significance to you is the information that it stores, processes, and provides. In order to fully understand computer capabilities and thus get the most out of a computer, let us review how the computer stores information.

What Is on the Disk?

The data about your business is stored on the disk in logical groupings called "files." Information about customers will be in one file, inventory in another, and so on. There are two primary types of files: master files and transaction files. The distinction between the two is important and helps allay a common fear that the disk will "fill up," or run out of storage space.

Master Files:

Figure 2-1 illustrates a Customer Master File. This is an abbreviated version, for an actual Customer Master File would contain all the pertinent data about your customers: name, address, telephone number, contact, terms, pricing code, salesman, credit limit, amount due, month-to-date and year-to-date sales, and so on.

The information about one customer is called a "record." Within a record, each unique piece of data (such as amount due or pricing code) is called a "field."

The records within a master file are usually kept in a logical sequence, such as alphabetical, or by customer number. From time to time, however,

Figure 2-1
CUSTOMER MASTER FILE

Index:		
Name		**Record No.**
ABC Marine		1
Ajax Industries		2
Barker & Co.		5
Carlson, Ltd.		3
Donovan, Int'l.		4
Records:		
Name	**Address**	**Balance Due, $** **YTD Sales, $**
ABC Marine	Santa Ana, Calif.	1,000 5,000
Ajax Industries	Carmel, Calif.	1,250 7,500
Carlson, Ltd.	San Diego, Calif.	600 3,500
Donovan, Int'l.	Atlanta, Ga.	835 10,600
Barker & Co.	Santa Monica, Calif.	250 250

you will have new customers who must be added to the file. Since the computer can't physically split your file to squeeze in the new customer, it puts the new record at the end of the file. However, please note from Figure 2-1 that a master file has an index, or table of contents, which is in alphabetical sequence and points to the actual location of each record.

What does this index mean? If you want an alphabetical listing of your customers, the computer can produce it even though the records are not actually in that sequence. If you want to see the status of a particular customer, you input the name and the computer scans the index, finds the location of the record, and fetches it immediately. With an index, you can locate a record in 1 to 2 seconds; without one, it might take several minutes. The index is the key to rapid and efficient retrieval of your data.

Transaction Files:

Transaction files, as the term might indicate, are temporary files which hold current business activity. For example, you input orders on a daily basis. They are held on disk in a transaction file and used to produce pick lists, invoices, and so on. Once the orders have been filled and invoiced, master files are updated to reflect the activity: Accounts Receivable balances and sales figures go up, Inventory stock levels go down. Then the transaction file is erased, leaving room for additional orders. Your disk, therefore, will not fill up unless your business really grows and you are storing more customers, more orders per day, and so on.

Updating:

As was mentioned earlier, the disk provides the computer's permanent storage. The data on the disk is retained in the computer and is continually available to you. However, the data is not set in concrete, it is written magnetically and can be changed and rewritten. Thus when a customer moves, you can enter the new address and the computer will write it over the old one. As a result of today's transactions, a customer may owe $1,000 instead of $500. The computer will again write it over the top. If the new number is larger than the old one, that's okay, because the size of each field is set up to accommodate the largest number you might want to store.

Sorting:

As mentioned, master files are usually maintained in logical sequence—probably alphabetical or by customer number. At times, you will want the data resequenced to make it more meaningful. For instance, you may want to list your customers according to the size of their overdue Accounts Receivable. The computer leaves the original file intact, but creates a second version of the file with the records in the desired sequence. This "sorted" file is used for the desired report and then erased.

WHAT CAN YOU DO WITH ALL THIS DATA?

You can now visualize the type of data which can be stored and appreciate its integrity—always current as of today's transactions. Your master files can be used to provide an infinite number of outputs for a variety of purposes. Many examples are laid out in the chapter on computer benefits, but you should first understand five basic types of outputs.

Operational Documents:

These are produced as a direct result of transactions you have entered and include: invoices, payroll checks, accounts payable checks, and so on. They are similar to what you would produce manually, but they require less of your time. A by-product of producing these is that your master files are updated thus allowing the creation of all the following outputs.

Reference Reports:

These are lists of entire files which might be used for control purposes or simply for reference. For example, every time you send statements, you will want an aged trial balance listing every account in alphabetic sequence together with the amount owed. After each payroll, you will print a recap of each check written. These can be filed and referred to in the future if a question arises.

Exception Reports:

These are management reports which call your attention only to items needing your attention. You might list customers with a delinquent balance due or inventory items needing reordering. The computer's logic capability allows it to sift through your entire inventory file looking for those items meeting a predetermined set of criteria (such as on-hand stock below minimum). It selects these "exception" items for printing so you don't have to wade through reams of unnecessary paper.

Ranking Reports:

These management reports are the most valuable of all. You can specify what is to appear on a ranking report as well as the sequence in which it is to appear. This is really letting the computer work for you and provide you with something exceptionally meaningful. A ranking report might be a list of your entire inventory, ranked by profit, or it might be a list of only those items which haven't moved in six months, ranked by the dollar value of the quantity on hand. The report is sequenced so that your own time is optimized— the most significant information is first on the list.

Inquiries:

An inquiry is a direct request to the computer for specific information. Thanks to the master file index, the computer can rapidly locate any record and display it for you on the screen. You may want to see the status of an account, an inventory item, a plant work order, a salesman, and so on.

What Does all This Mean to You?

The computer can perform tasks and provide information to improve your business operations and enhance your ability to manage. Further ideas on the specific uses of a computer are contained in the next chapter.

3

Why Should You Get a Computer?

Financial analysts seem to agree on the five major reasons that small businesses fail. These are all essentially management problems and they are, in order:

1. Low sales
2. Poor collection procedures
3. Too many fixed assets
4. Too much of the wrong inventory
5. High operating expenses

Each of these problems, with the exception of too many fixed assets, can be addressed and improved with the proper use of a computer. Some case studies which will show you how some very successful businesses have used computers follow.

LOW SALES

At the end of each month, many businesses without computers manually prepare one or two sketchy reports showing total gross sales by product class, customer class, sales representatives, or geographic territory. These sales analysis reports are time consuming to prepare and, therefore, are often late. Still, they can be useful in preparing marketing strategies.

With a computer, your sales figures are up to date with each order. Therefore, as a simple by-product of processing orders on a computer, you can have all the sales statistics you need with no additional labor expended. One of the key advantages of a computer is its ability to sort, sift, and summarize information for you—saving you hours of tedious work. Only your imagination and the size of your computer limit the information available to you. Here are some examples of creative sales analysis on a small business computer:

An office supply distributor got a quarterly report for each sales rep listing all of his customers with comparative figures on sales year-to-date this year versus last year. Sales variances of more than 20 percent were flagged. The owner of the business reviewed this report personally with each rep and together they set quarterly goals for increasing sales to selected customers. (See Figure 3-1.)

Result: Sales increased 35 percent the first quarter and doubled by the end of 1 year.

A candy distributor produced a report showing sales by product class for each of its customers. The report included the profit each store had made selling candy at the suggested retail price. The sales reps reviewed this report with each store and pointed out the money the store could make by carrying additional lines of products.

Result: Sales increased by 80 percent within 12 months.

A distributor of imported sunglasses produced a report for each sales rep, ranking his customers by gross profit. He classified the customers as A, B, C, or D accounts according to potential. The distributor determined how many calls per year should be made on each class of customer and redistributed the sales representatives' time accordingly. (See Figure 3-2.)

Result: Within a year, sales had increased 65 percent.

A mail order business put in a computer largely to analyze sales by source in order to evaluate the effectiveness of its advertising.

Result: Sales increased 45 percent while advertising costs decreased 10 percent.

An industrial supply distributor listed all products in order of profit contribution. He redirected his sales promotions and commission plan to emphasize the high profit items and repriced the low profit items. (See Figure 3-2.)

Result: Gross profit increased by 55 prcent.

A candy and tobacco distributor listed lost sales (orders that could not be filled and were cancelled) by vendor. He reviewed this with his suppliers to "encourage" shorter and more reliable lead times and better service.

Result: Service improved and sales went up 35 percent.

Figure 3-1
COMPARATIVE SALES ANALYSIS REPORTS

9/30/82

Sales by Customer*

Customer Name	Last Order Date	Month-to-Date		Year-to-Date		
		Sales, $	Profit, $	Sales, $	Profit, $	Orders
Creative Industries						
This year	5/7/82	0	0	9,760	4,210	23
Last year		2,300	1,100	18,400	10,600	41
Lincoln International						
This year	6/15/82	0	0	11,450	5,700	17
Last year		1,700	850	16,800	9,950	29
Boswell, Inc.						
This year	8/14/82	0	0	13,412	6,390	22
Last year		1,300	658	15,621	8,920	31

*Sales this year versus last are compared for all customers. This report is printed in sequence by last order date.

9/30/82

Sales by Product Class†

Product Class	Month-to-Date				Year-to-Date			
	Sales, $	Cost, $	Profit, $	Change, %	Sales, $	Cost, $	Profit, $	Change, %
This year	10,390	5,300	5,090	25	80,750	40,300	40,450	14
Last year	8,116	4,100	4,016		71,900	36,500	35,400	
This year	8,150	4,500	3,650	33	72,600	37,000	35,600	17
Last year	6,500	3,800	2,700		63,400	33,000	30,400	

†Sales, cost, and profit this year versus last are compared for each product class. The percentage of change is printed for both month-to-date and year-to-date profit.

Figure 3-2
SALES RANKING REPORTS
All Reports Are Sequenced by Profit

Item Ranking

Rank	Product Number	Description	Sales, $	Profit, $	Profit, %	Units Sold
					Year-to-Date	
1	601-A	Widgets	16,609	8,311	100	7,500
2	17V-36	Midgets	14,825	6,720	83	923
3	81-92B	Didgets	13,050	6,150	89	3,060

Salesman Ranking

Rank	Salesman	Month-to-Date			Year-to-Date		
		No. Orders	Sales, $	Profit, $	No. Orders	Sales, $	Profit, $
1	Jones	37	11,600	4,990	296	123,800	46,000
2	Barlow	32	9,650	3,670	225	106,900	38,500

Customer Ranking

Salesman	Rank	Customer	Year-to-Date		
			No. Orders	Sales, $	Profit, %
Barlow	1	Creative Ind.	33	9,067	3,850
	2	Cal Marine	27	7,650	2,190
	3	Containers, Ltd.	22	6,890	1,740

A drug wholesaler put in a computer to improve service during order taking. Each order desk had a screen on it connected to the computer. As an order was processed, the order taker could commit stock, suggest alternate products if the item ordered was unavailable, recommend items that were on special, and so on. The information the computer supplied to the order takers made them appear more professional and allowed them to sell more products.

Result: Sales increased by 50 percent.

As you can see, with careful thought you can devise equally creative sales analysis reports for your business. Figures 3-1 through 3-3 illustrate some examples of computer produced sales analysis reports.

Figure 3-3
MORE DETAILED SALES ANALYSIS

Sales by Product Class Within Sales Rep				
Sales Rep	Product Class	Sales, $	Profit, $	Profit, %*
Bennion	1	810.90	348.75	76
	3	600.73	78.00	15
	8	1,620.95	411.89	33
	11	2,850.36	570.21	19
Braddock	1	4,360.20	1,373.50	46
	2	400.16	148.70	60
	3	750.90	300.90	66

*Calculated as a percentage of cost.

Sales by Item Within Customer						
Customer	Item No.	Units Sold	Sales, $	Cost, $	Profit, $	Profit, %*
Baugh Mfg.	601-2	201	4,163	2,580	1,583	61
	803-4B	178	2,090	1,361	729	53
	990-12	485	1,563	912	651	71
	1062-11	710	1,312	850	462	54
	1490-13	412	1,290	965	325	34

*Calculated as a percentage of cost.

POOR COLLECTION PROCEDURES

Most businesses prepare a month-end aging report listing outstanding Accounts Receivable. Some even invest the time to prepare this weekly or daily so they can take action quickly to collect delinquent amounts and hold orders for accounts that are not current. It is obviously time consuming to produce these reports manually and, what is worse, the reports themselves are not as helpful as they should be.

In this time of high interest rates, it is more difficult and, yet, more important than ever to promptly collect the money owed to you. With a computer, you can produce some very effective reports to assist with collections. Before we get into them, let us first review a point about computers.

As you know, a computer can read information very rapidly and resequence it so that the final report you read is most meaningful to you. For example, your customer accounts receivable records inside the computer memory are usually kept in account number or alphabetic sequence (just as they would be in a file drawer). However, the computer can resequence them according to the delinquent amount owed and print your aging report in that sequence. If you use this report to follow up by telephone, you will be tackling your worst problem first. According to a survey taken in the 1960s, businesses whose names begin with A have better payment records than those beginning with letters toward the end of the alphabet. Although the As are undoubtedly very fine folks, it appears the reason for this is that most aging reports are in alphabetic sequence and the As are hassled sooner and more often! Why not use your computer to help you hassle the ones who owe the most and are not paying?

Here are some examples of creative and effective collection procedures with a computer. (In all cases the results are expressed in terms of collection period, which is the average number of days it takes a business to collect its Accounts Receivable.)

A manufacturer of surgical equipment produced a weekly list of invoices over $500 that were also over 40 days old. The report included company name, contact, telephone number, the invoice number, date, and amount. This was used for telephone follow-up. (See Figure 3-4.)

Result: The company's collection period dropped from 68 to 45 days.

A sporting goods distributor produced a weekly report of customers with delinquent amounts of over $1,000, sequenced by amount due. He used this report for telephone follow-up and found for the first time that he was getting in touch with all the critical customers in a timely fashion. (See Figure 3-5.)

Result: His collection period dropped from 53 to 42 days.

A manufacturer of air conditioning equipment put in a computer to do Order Processing. If an order came in for a customer with any amount due that was over 60 days delinquent, company personnel held the order. They then listed these accounts, called the person who had placed the order, explained that unfortunately they could not fill it until the bill was paid, and asked him to see his own accounts payable clerk to encourage payment.

Result: The firm's collection period fell from an incredible 78 days to 48 days.

An importer of gift items produced a monthly aging report for each of its sales reps. In order to encourage their help in collecting, the company paid them additional commissions if they could reduce the over-60-day amount. Conversely, if the over-60 grew, the importer reduced the sales reps commissions. (See Figure 3-6.)

Result: At the end of 3 months, the firm's collection period fell from 67 to 48 days. (And lest you wonder if this diverted the reps from selling, sales went up simultaneously.)

An office supply distributor with an excellent accounts receivable position decided that this position could be even better. They offered the standard

Figure 3-4
ACCOUNTS RECEIVABLE
Exception Reports

Customers Over Credit Limit						
Customer Name	Contact Tel No.	Credit Limit, $	Total Due, $	Current, $	Over 30, $	Over 60, $
ABC Sales	Joe 454-1888	3,500	4,300	2,200	2,100	0
Baker Ind.	Sally 276-4400	2,500	3,150	1,275	1,800	75
Carlton, Ltd.	Barbara 871-4351	3,000	3,650	1,150	1,700	800

9/30/82							
			Invoices Over 40 Days				
Customer Name	Invoices	Date/ Age	Amount, $	Avg. Number Days to Pay	Contact	Tel No.	
ABC Sales	12371	8/15	2,100	47	Joe	454-1888	
Baker Ind.	11321	8/19	1,800	52	Sally	276-4400	
	12582	7/15	575				
Carlton Ind.	11422	7/18	800	59	Barbara	821-4351	
	12491	8/18	700				
	12516	8/20	1,000				

discount of 2 percent for payment within 10 days. Their computer produced a daily list of customers who were within 1 day on either side of the discount date. The distributor then called these accounts to remind them that if they put the check in the mail that day, they would not miss the discount. Those who had just missed it were told to drop the check in the mail and go ahead and take the discount.

Result: Their customers loved the service and their collection period fell from 46 to 37 days.

A manufacturer of sporting goods was concerned about damaging customer good will by sending delinquency notices. The firm decided to go ahead with the notices but to personalize them by having the computer print: "I am a computer and I know you owe us X amount. If you will pay me, I promise not to turn you over to a people!"

Result: The manufacturer's collection period dropped from 65 to 48 days and the computer got 2 thank you notes!

Figure 3-5
ACCOUNTS RECEIVABLE
Ranking Reports

Delinquent Customer Ranking						
Customer	Tel No.	Balance Due, $	Past Due, $	Over 30, $	Over 60, $	Over 90, $
Mercury Int.	621-3100	3,250	2,780	1,325	1,140	315
Adams Motors	771-1896	2,640	2,410	1,210	500	700
Stevens Marine	372-1648	2,830	2,170	1,450	720	
Smith & Sons	374-5211	2,340	1,890	840	550	500
Creative Ent.	432-1616	2,190	1,650	620	520	510
Essex, Ltd.	299-2100	2,880	1,520	760	440	320
Cole & Co.	297-2238	2,980	1,250	350	660	240
Kolve Co.	681-7542	1,560	1,220	410	310	500
Brune Bld.	641-9141	1,280	1,180	310	350	520
Biker Co.	245-3131	1,309	1,110	380	290	440
Marvin Whls.	419-8100	1,375	1,050	320	320	410
Fab Dist.	256-2000	1,590	930	610	150	170

Average No. Days to Pay				
Customer	Tel No.	Avg. No. Days to Pay	Total Due, $	Past Due, $
Mercury Int.	621-3100	61	3,250	2,780
Stevens Mar.	372-1648	59	2,830	2,170
Essex Ltd.	299-2100	52	2,880	1,520

An industrial supply distributor developed a unique approach to measuring the profitability of each of its customers by taking into consideration their payment habits. It was determined that it cost 36 percent per year to carry the company's Accounts Receivable. This percentage was the sum of an 18 percent cost of money and an 18 percent administrative collection expense. The 36 percent was then divided by 365 days per year and it was determined that each day an invoice went unpaid it cost 0.1 percent. The computer calculated the age of each invoice as it was paid and computed the collection expense associated with that invoice (0.1 percent of the invoice amount for each day it was unpaid). This expense was calculated for each customer and subtracted from the gross profit generated by that account. Then the customers were ranked according to profit contribution and it was found that some of the best customers weren't the best profit contributors! This operation would have been extremely cumbersome to perform manually but it was quite simple for the computer. This distributor actually eliminated some customers where he was losing money and started charging a service charge for unpaid balances.

Result: His collection period dropped from 71 to 47 days.

Figure 3-6
ACCOUNTS RECEIVABLE
Reports by Sales Representative

Past Due Accounts Receivable by Sales Representative					
Sales Rep	Customer	Total Due, $	Current, $	Over 30, $	Over 60, $
Jones	Adams Motors	2,640	230	1,210	1,200
	Creative Ent.	2,190	540	620	1,030
	Essex, Ltd.	2,880	1,360	760	760
	Kolve Co.	1,560	340	410	810
	Marvin Whls.	1,375	325	320	730
		10,645	2,795	3,320	4,530

Credit Holds by Rep					
Sales Rep	Customer	Credit Limit, $	Total Due, $	Past Due, $	Tel No.
Smith	Mercury Int.	2,500	3,250	2,780	621-3100
	Stevens Mar.	2,000	2,830	2,170	372-1648
	Smith & Sons	1,800	2,340	1,890	347-5211
	Cole & Co.	2,500	2,980	1,250	297-2238
	Brune Bld.	1,000	1,280	1,180	641-9141

A travel agent found that when he put in a computer to manage his Accounts Receivable he was able to prove to his bank that his control had improved.

Result: The interest rate on the money he borrowed dropped half a percentage point.

A job shop got a computer and for the first time found it practical to apply finance charges to delinquent balances.

Result: They earned $3,700 on their Accounts Receivable the first year.

A law firm got a computer primarily to address Accounts Receivable. On their manual system, they got an Aging report only once a year. Their collection period was 6 months long. They used the computer to list delinquent clients by attorney. At weekly staff meetings, each attorney had to explain the status of each delinquent client.

Result: The attorneys (or their secretaries) followed up with their clients and pushed for payment. Within 60 days, the collection period had improved 50 percent.

Figures 3-4 through 3-7 illustrate some of these reports. A little imagination and good sound management led to outstanding results for these companies.

Figure 3-7
ACCOUNTS RECEIVABLE
Inquiry Screens

9/30/82				
	Open-Item Inquiry			
Customer No: 1012			Name: Mercury Int.	
Invoice No.	**Trans**	**Date**	**Amount, $**	**Balance, $**
10231	Inv	6/20/82	460	
10231	Pmt	7/30/82	100	360
10450	Inv	7/17/82	610	610
10890	Inv	7/25/82	780	
10890	Pmt	9/10/82	250	530
11990	Inv	8/15/82	1,325	1,325
12120	Inv	9/17/82	470	470
Current	**Over 30**	**Over 60**	**Over 90**	**Total**
$470	$1,325	$1,140	$360	$3,295

Customer Status Inquiry				
Customer No: 1012			Name: Mercury Int.	
Current	**Over 30**	**Over 60**	**Over 90**	**Total**
$470	$1,325	$1,140	$315	$3,250
Avg. Days to Pay: 61				
	Sales	**Cost**		**Profit**
MTD	470	310		160
YTD	8,890	5,240		3,650
PYR	11,910	6,950		4,960

TOO MANY FIXED ASSETS

A computer can assist you with fixed asset accounting, depreciation schedules, and so forth, but it can't really help you unload them if you've acquired too many. (The unkind among you may be thinking that the computer is just another capital asset, but remember all its benefits!)

TOO MUCH WRONG INVENTORY

No area of your business has more benefit potential than inventory. A major computer company surveyed 100 customers who had put Inventory Control on their computers. The results were staggering. Service had increased 10 to 30 percent (in other words, stockouts and lost sales had been reduced) and at the same time inventory investment had declined 10 to 50 percent. And it was not done with mirrors! The key was in rebalancing the inventory toward items that would sell while lowering overall dollars spent.

In this time of enormous interest rates, it is vital to watch the level of inventory investment quite closely and make every dollar count. Experts within the distribution industry believe that it now costs 30 to 40 percent of the value of your inventory to carry it. Carrying costs include the interest on the money, taxes, insurance, obsolescence, shrinkage, handling costs, and opportunity cost (if your money is tied up in a product that is not turning, there is an opportunity cost associated). Some people even estimate that the carrying cost in certain industries is as high as 50 percent. If you can reduce your inventory by only $10,000, you may be saving as much as $5,000 per year.

Every business has items that have had birthdays in the warehouse (1 year on the shelf with no sale). Other items may be selling, but at the rate they sell you may have a 100-year supply. And of course, there are those popular and profitable products that are gone and back ordered. The computer can be an incredibly powerful tool in helping you identify problem areas in time to fix them.

A computer can tell you as of the last order, what you have in stock and your overall inventory investment. On a manual system, it is very easy for a $200,000 inventory to sneak up to $250,000. If cash or credit becomes tight, you can always fix the problem by not ordering more. That will bring your investment back down, but what does it do to your inventory balance? You now have all of the items that don't sell and none of the ones that do. With a computer, you have the information to manage your inventory investment wisely.

Using the computer's sorting and selection capabilities, you can produce exception reports to do the following:

- Identify items that fall below a minimum or reorder point as soon as they do, so that you can avoid a stockout.
- Identify items which are increasingly in demand, thus suggesting a change in reordering policy.
- List products which haven't moved in a specified period of time, so you can hold a firesale.
- List items where the number of months supply (based on the current sales rate) is greater than a minimum, thus allowing you either to promote the products or to get rid of them.
- Identify items where sales are declining so you can slow down your reordering.
- Identify items on order which are overdue so that you can expedite them.

By letting the computer flag those items which are either slow- or fast-moving, you have an opportunity to take action quickly.

Ranking reports, which list your entire inventory according to factors of your choice, are enormously valuable. Most of you are familiar with the 80/20 rule—20 percent of your products account for 80 percent of your sales. (Similarly, 20 percent of your customers account for 80 percent of your sales.) Identifying the top 20 percent of your inventory lets you know where to put your emphasis when it comes to evaluating reordering policy or marketing strategies.

In a matter of minutes, the computer can sort your inventory in order of sales year-to-date, cost, or profit allowing you to print a report ranking your items accordingly. This will show you very clearly which are your most and least significant products and, thus, which ones to spend your time controlling.

If you need to operate on a more sophisticated level, you can use a computer to forecast sales and reorder products based on the projections. For a distributor, the computer can determine how much needs to be ordered and when to place the order so that you can optimize your investment and still meet a minimum service level. For a manufacturer, the computer can project future material requirements based on sales forecasts for finished goods and estimated spare parts usage. These computer applications are Inventory Management and Material Requirements Planning. Neither should be attempted until you have had a computer doing basic inventory accounting for at least 2 years (so that you can base your forecasting criteria on a reasonable approximation of your firm's past history).

Here are some inventory success stories:

A different auto parts distributor used the computer to produce a vendor reordering report listing items whose stock on hand had just dropped to the point where it would not last through the expected supplier lead time (based on the current sales rate). (See Figure 3-8.)

Result: Their stockouts were cut in half and their total inventory investment went down nearly 30 percent.

A sporting goods distributor had always used a simple "min-max" inventory reordering system. When an item's on-hand quantity fell below the established minimum, they ordered up to the maximum quantity. This worked well for a short time, but in an industry with both seasonal as well as high trend products, the validity of their minimum and maximum figures rapidly deteriorated. They did not have time on a manual system to continually reevaluate the figures. Using a computer, they were able to print out several periods of sales history as well as the forecast sales quantity through the expected lead time. If the forecast was greater or less than the established minimum by more than a certain percent, the item was flagged for their review. They also classified products according to season and reviewed them only at the appropriate time. (See Figure 3-8.)

Result: Their inventory investment was reduced by 25 percent, while service increased 10 percent.

An importer of women's shoes had an enormous stockout problem until they put in their computer. They had been ordering huge quantities to maintain a buffer stock, since it took so long to replenish their inventory. After using the computer for 1 complete year, they began some rudimentary forecasting of sales. It was enough to allow more careful product planning. (See Figure 3-8.)

Result: Stockouts dropped from 40 percent of all items ordered to about 15 percent and their inventory went down 10 percent.

An auto parts distributor with 36,000 items had a year-end opportunity to return up to $40,000 worth of parts to one of their suppliers. The questions were, which parts and how many of each? They used their computer to calculate the number of months supply on hand for every item (on-hand quantity divided by average monthly sales) and print the items in sequence with the most overstocked item first. The report showed the item number and description as well as the number of months supply and dollar value of the on-hand inventory. The first page displayed items that were stocked to infinity since sales had been zero! (See Figure 3-10.)

Result: With that report, it took less than 30 minutes to decide what to return.

An industrial supply distributor, after using his computer for 6 months, printed a list of all items that had not sold. He found that he had more than $40,000 in "dead" inventory for which he was paying at least $15,000 per year carrying cost. Although it may sound unbelievable, he actually held an auction to unload it all. (He claims the sale went so well, he was tempted to haul out his good inventory!) (See Figure 3-10.)

Result: He saved the carrying cost of $15,000 and made $27,000 on the auction!

A motorcycle parts distributor put in a computer to flag parts that needed reordering. His parts manager said the comptuer was not only more efficient than he had been, but had saved him so much time that he was able to do successfully those things that require a human being—such as calling vendors to inquire about shipments and negotiate better prices or improved service. (See Figure 3-10.)

Result: Their business doubled and the inventory investment did not increase at all!

A plumbing distributor with over 20,000 parts installed a computer and was able to do some inventory analysis for the first time. Through the use of ranking reports that listed his items according to annual profit, he reestablished the stocking levels for his critical items. At first, his inventory went up as he was understocked on some parts. Over time, he reduced his stock in other areas by using sales promotions. (See Figure 3-11.)

Result: After 6 months, his inventory was down 30 percent and service was up 15 percent.

A manufacturer who had a problem of incomplete finished goods because of critical parts shortages put Material Requirements Planning (MRP) on his computer.

Result: He improved customer service and increased the number of on-time shipments from 60 percent to 91 percent.

A manufacturer who had to contend with parts piled up on the plant floor, scarce floor space, and many parts shortages at the same time put MRP on his computer.

Result: Component inventory levels dropped 20 percent and customer service improved 10 percent.

Computer-produced inventory reports gave these businesses the information they needed to exercise excellent management skills. Figures 3-8 through 3-11 are examples of such reports.

Figure 3-8
INVENTORY REORDERING REPORTS

Stock Status Report							
Item No.*	Description	Reorder Point	Qty on Hand	Allocated	Back Ordered	On Order	Available
901-6	Ceramic trays	24	11	0	0	24	35
1016-30	Tile planters	36	7	0	0	24	31†
1118-21	Decorative plate	12	0	0	3	12	9†
1321-75	Crystal vase	24	3	3	2	24	22†

*All items may be listed or only those needing reordering.

†Indicates available stock is below reorder point, necessitating a new order.

Inventory Movement Analysis		Sales						
Item No.	Description	This Mo.	Last Mo.	Avg of 6 Mo.	Lead Time, Mo.	Expected Usage	Avail. Stock	Reorder Point
901-6	Ceramic Trays	2	1	3	2	6	35	24
1016-30	Tile planters	3	5	6	2	12	31	36
1118-21	Decorative plate	6	4	5	2.5	13	9	12
1321-75	Crystal vase	1	1	4	1	4	22	24

Note: Expected usage is average monthly sales times the number of months lead time. Quantity on hand should not fall below this figure. This report illustrates how a predetermined reorder point can become invalid as the sales rate moves up or down. The Stock Status Report would have us reorder items 1016-30 and 1321-75. The Inventory Movement Analysis Report b shows declining sales for these items and we would probably not reorder them.

Figure 3-9
INVENTORY FINANCIAL REPORTS

		Recommended Orders by Vendor					
Vendor No.	Item No.	Description	Reorder	Available	Sugg. Order Qty.	Unit Cost, $	Order Cost, $
1	101	Picture frames	24	11	24	2	48
	106	Ceramic bells	48	3	60	1	60
	111	Vases	60	21	48	3	144
							Total $252

Note: This tells you the expense involved with all of your reordering recommendations.

		Inventory Valuation				
Item No.	Description	Qty on Hand	Unit Cost, $	On-Hand Value	Qty on Order	On-Order Value, $
101	Picture frames	11	2	22	24	48
106	Ceramic bells	3	1	3	60	60
111	Vases	21	3	63	48	144
					Total	$252

Note: At a glance you see your entire inventory investment with the details for each item.

Figure 3-10
INVENTORY EXCEPTION REPORTS

		Recommended Returns						
Item No.	Description	Last Sale	Qty on Hand	Sales MTD	Sales YTD	Avg. Mo. Sales	Avg. Mo. Supply	Value on Hand, $
1518	Ceramic lamps	5/12/82	37	0	7	1	37	496
1762	Pleated shades	2/21/81	12	0	0	0	Infinite	374
2081	Daisy watch	3/18/81	43	0	3	3	129	819

Note: This report clearly indicates where you are overstocked.

		Overdue Shipments					
Vendor Tel No.	Item No.	Qty on Hand	Back Orders	Available	Qty on Order	Date Ord.	Expected Del
Mermaid Marine (213) 276-1888	1096	0	36	(36)	60	8/1/82	9/1/82
	1212	3	0	3	48	8/1/82	9/1/82
	1316	0	13	(13)	24	8/1/82	9/1/82

Note: This information can be used to press suppliers for delivery.

Figure 3-11
INVENTORY RANKING REPORTS

		Item Ranking by Annual Cost					
Rank	Item No.	Description	Annual Cost, $	Accum. Cost, $	% of Total	Accum. % of Total	% of Items Counted
1	9034	Brass beds	15,633	15,633	3.3	3.3	.03
2	8714	Iron carts	14,890	30,523	2.9	6.2	.06
3	1649B	Oak coffee tables	12,670	43,193	2.5	8.7	.09
:	:	:	:	:	:	:	:
3068	154AB	Brass lamps		498,650	0.01	100.	100.

Note: Not only does this report indicate your key, high-cost items, but as you accumulate 20 percent of the items counted, you will see 80 percent of your cost accumulated— the "80/20" rule.

		Item Profitability						
Item No.	Description	Avg. Cost, $	Qty Break	Prices, $	Profit, $	%	Year-to-Date Profit, $	%
7090	Iron wheels	4.50	24	6.50	2.00	44	5,060	37
			48	6.00	1.50	33		
			96	5.50	1.00	27		
1690	Iron trays	2.20	24	3.30	1.10	50	4,860	35
			60	3.00	.80	36		
			120	2.70	.50	23		

Note: This report may be ranked on year-to-date profit or profit percent. It allows you to review your prices as costs change to ensure that you are making adequate margins.

HIGH OPERATING EXPENSE

Declining productivity growth is one of our country's major concerns, yet it is likely that when historians write of this period of American business, they will note that the computer was the most significant productivity aid ever developed. Properly used, it can provide information to make all employees more productive: clerks, warehouse workers, manufacturing personnel, salesmen, accountants, and management.

Rarely does a business replace employees with a computer. You might well argue that operating expense is increased by the additional equipment expense. Yet the benefit of the computer is in the increased productivity of your employees, allowing you to grow without adding people. You will also be able to assign your people responsibilities they previously had no time for.

And since normal attrition will reduce your staff, you may find that you don't need to replace them.

A brief overview of the productivity benefits a computer can provide your people follows.

Clerical Aids

Clerical time in all accounting areas is cut by at least 50 percent. With Order Processing, the basic information about your customers (name, address, terms, etc.) and your products (description, unit of measure, prices, etc.) is entered into the computer only once. It is then automatically retrieved for each order and invoice. Your clerk need only type into the computer the unique information for each order (customer identification, part numbers, quantities). The machine performs all calculations and prints the order, picking list or manufacturing work order, bill of lading, and invoice. Inventory, Accounts Receivable, and sales figures are automatically updated using no clerical time whatsoever.

In addition to the obvious time savings with this approach, the documents produced are more accurate and impressive in appearance than those which are prepared manually.

Word Processing, an application which is now available on all microcomputers and some minicomputers, is also a significant clerical productivity tool. With a Word Processing program, your computer can store commonly used text: letters, contracts, proposals, and so on. With a few keystrokes, these documents can be customized and printed afresh for new clients or customers. This eliminates all of the pain and lost time required to retype them in their entirety.

Most clerical workers find greater job satisfaction when they start to use a computer. The mundane tasks such as retyping old and familiar letters and routine accounting chores (looking up prices, calculating extensions and invoice totals, typing, posting, and so forth) are eliminated. They find that they can get more work done in a day and that the pressure is reduced. They also feel the satisfaction that comes with learning and mastering a new skill. An informal survey of trained computer users did not reveal one who didn't prefer computer to manual methods.

From your point of view, your operating expenses should level off while your sales increase. Many companies have grown between 30 and 200 percent without adding to their clerical staffs.

A chain saw distributor has two clerks and a computer. He believes that without the computer, he would need an administrative staff of ten.

A liquor distributor has grown 45 percent and has 1 less employee since putting in his computer.

A job shop has doubled, gives better service, and is down one employee.

A beer distributor tripled in size without adding people.

We could go on and on.

Warehouse Aids

Picking slips produced on a computer are more legible so that fewer errors are made and picking efficiency is increased. The items on each order may be printed in warehouse location sequence, greatly improving picking productivity.

A food distributor assigned aisle and bin locations to each product and printed picking lists in warehouse sequence.

Result: 3 warehouse employees now do the work once done by 5 and sales have increased 30 percent.

A hardware distributor reorganized his warehouse according to item movement with the fast selling products near the shipping dock. He then printed all pick lists in location sequence.

Result: Sales have increased 80 percent and he is down 1 person in the warehouse.

Computers are also valuable time savers during physical inventories. They will list the items to be counted in warehouse sequence, prepare discrepancy reports, and rapidly compute the value of your on-hand inventory.

Manufacturing Aids

Sophisticated manufacturing applications such as Material Requirements Planning, Production Control, Forecasting, and Capacity Planning are usually not attempted until a company has used a computer for years. The implementation of these applications requires tremendous discipline and clean paperwork procedures. However, the benefits are enormous: increased productivity of people and machines, improved planning, and increased profitability.

For manufacturers and job shops starting with their first computer, there are also terrific productivity benefits. Paperwork is simplified with Bills of Material, Routings, Product Costing, and Job Costing on the computer.

A manufacturer of motorcycle parts put his Bills of Material on the computer.

Result: He was able to recost his inventory in 2 hours instead of 3 weeks. His prices kept up with inflation and he played more golf.

A job shop put Routings and Job Status on a computer.

Result: They saved 2 weeks per month in clerical time and increased plant equipment utilization by 25 percent.

Sales Aids

Sales analysis reports were discussed at length in the first section of this chapter. Two types of reports are especially helpful in increasing sales productivity:

1. Customer ranking reports (on sales or profits) to assist in rebalancing sales priorities.
2. Comparative reports showing customer sales this year versus last. These give the sales rep valuable information to use in a sales call.

Accounting and Financial Management Aids:

Monthly and annual financial reporting is an automatic by-product of operational accounting, including Accounts Payable, Inventory and Accounts Receivable. Income statements, balance sheets, budget reporting are all available on demand. This saves hours of accounting time and ensures that you have the information you need when you need it.

Management Aids:

Perhaps of greatest significance to managers and owners of small businesses are the areas in which a computer can assist management in becoming more productive. Many busy executives are concerned that the computer will bury them in reports, but a properly established computer system should do the opposite. The exception reports and ranking reports that were discussed should enable you to identify profitable and unprofitable areas of your business or practice and to target your own efforts to the areas which count.

Some exceptional computer programs designed specifically to be used by or for business executives are now on the market. Curiously, there are more of these currently available on the small microcomputers than on the larger minicomputers. These executive-oriented programs include:

Financial Planning or Electronic Spreadsheet Programs

Many microcomputers have been sold on the strength of this program alone. It allows you to build a financial model of your business over time (perhaps 1 year, perhaps 5). You can vary such figures as sales forecasts, prices, and expenses and see the result to your bottom line. This is a fantastic business planning tool and allows you to play "what if" with a minimum of effort. Business executives who use this type of program say they would *never* be able to do detailed planning without the help of a computer.

Data Base/Report Writer Programs

This is another exceptional tool for the business executive. It allows you to set up an electronic filing system of anything you want to keep track of. Furthermore, this can be indexed and cross-indexed multiple ways so you can quickly find what you need. For example, a lawyer or his assistant might make a computer entry for each document in his files. The entry could include client name, other parties involved, matter number, date, subject, secondary subjects, comments, and the location of the document. This entry can be indexed by any of these elements, thus allowing the lawyer to quickly get a list of all documents relating to a specific client, matter, or subject.

Time Management Programs

For the executive with a packed and constantly changing schedule, a computer can make an excellent administrative assistant. All appointments, deadlines, follow-up tasks, and to-dos can be logged in the computer as they come up. Then each day's calendar and to-do list can be printed quickly and neatly.

All of these programs are aids to make us more efficient in these busy and competitive times. Your mind is your business's greatest asset. A computer can give you more time to use it.

4

Will Your Computer Pay for Itself?

The management benefits of a computer should be evident at this point. But the next issues are: How do the benefits translate into dollars and does the computer pay for itself? This chapter will show you techniques for measuring benefit potential in hard dollars. The material is organized in the same benefit categories we discussed in the last chapter. Following a short discussion of techniques are some worksheets you can use to quantify your potential savings.

INCREASING SALES:

Will you be able to increase your sales by using the information provided by your computer? This is the most difficult area in which to project a concrete dollars and cents benefit. Some companies double and triple sales and give the credit to the computer, but only you can estimate what your growth might be.

IMPROVING ACCOUNTS RECEIVABLE COLLECTIONS:

There are four distinct financial benefits associated with automating Accounts Receivable:

1. Improving or shortening your collection period, thus improving cash flow and reducing interest expense.

2. Charging a service charge on delinquent accounts.
3. Reducing your bad debts.
4. Obtaining bank loans (or improving your relationship with your bank).

The important questions are: How much can you improve your collections and what is that worth to you?

A common technique for measuring the benefit of improved collection is called Collection Period Analysis. Your collection period is the average number of days it takes you to collect your accounts. You compute this by dividing your annual sales by 365 to get average daily sales. You then divide your outstanding Accounts Receivable by your average daily sales to get the number of days outstanding or collection period.

Now, how much can this be reduced with a computer? What is realistic? Dun and Bradstreet publishes a document which is extremely useful in this regard. It is called Key Business Ratios and it can be used to compare your business results with those of your competitors. They survey several businesses within each industry and publish mean, high-mean, and low-mean figures for a variety of significant business indicators. For example, they may look at 100 electrical distributors and rank them from best to worst on such things as collection period, inventory turns, and so on, publishing three figures for each business indicator. (The mean is the company in the middle, the high-mean is midway between the mean and the top, the low-mean is midway between the mean and the bottom.) If you compare your collection period with the figures for your industry, you can get a handle on the improvement potential. Using a computer, you should clearly be able to do as well as the mean and perhaps as well as the high-mean.

What does this do for your pocketbook? After you estimate the number of days you can shave from your collection period, multiply the days times your daily sales. This tells you the increased cash that will be available. The interest you will save on this cash is a direct Before Tax benefit.

After you reduce your collection period, you will obviously still have some delinquent accounts. Charging a service charge on these is another potential benefit. (This can be done manually, but is much easier with a computer.) You may reduce your collection period to, say, 42 days. If your terms are net 30, there are still 12 days worth of sales which are overdue. The benefit would be 12 times your average daily sales times the annual service percent you will charge. Many businesses figure that 50 percent of this is collectible.

The next Accounts Receivable benefit is in the area of bad debt reduction. You can figure on reducing bad debts with the additional control a computer will bring you. Some businesses have experienced 20 to 50 percent reductions.

Finally, your bank may reduce your interest rate if you have computerized your Accounts Receivable. If so, you can compute your annual interest savings.

Improving Inventory Control

The two seemingly at-odds inventory benefits are:

1. Reducing inventory investment and carrying costs
2. Improving service (reducing stockouts and lost sales)

The previous chapter illustrated some of the techniques for improving your inventory management. But at this point, you might be asking how much can you reduce inventory investment and maintain service? Many business executives will project a percentage reduction just based on gut feel or by asking other businesses what they have experienced. "If I had up-to-date inventory numbers, I know I could save 10 percent or 20 percent, or 30 percent." This has been done enough times so that a conservative projection can safely be made.

If you do not feel comfortable with the gut feel approach, Dun and Bradstreet again provides a technique. They publish mean, high-mean, and low-mean inventory turns for each industry. You can compute your own turns by dividing annual sales by average inventory investment. Compare this with the figures for your industry and decide the number of turns you can realistically achieve. If you divide your annual sales by the new projected number of turns, you determine your new inventory investment. The difference between the old and new inventory levels will be your inventory savings. As stated in the last chapter, the carrying cost you will save will be 25 to 40 percent of the inventory reduction.

Improved service, or reduction in lost sales, is more difficult to project. First, you need to estimate the dollars you are currently losing due to stockouts. Then you need to estimate how much you can improve on this. Many businesses are losing between 5 and 30 percent of their annual sales due to lack of inventory availability. It is realistic to believe you can cut this loss (perhaps by 25 to 50 percent).

Reducing operating expenses and increasing productivity

A computer will directly displace certain expenses:

- Current equipment and/or maintenance costs
- Service Bureau charges
- Some outside bookkeeping fees
- Clerical, plant and/or warehouse overtime expense

Additionally, accounting operations will be streamlined so that your people can be used for additional projects and your business can grow without adding people. Certain savings should also be realized through the improved accuracy of billing and shipping.

Presented in Figure 4-1 are worksheets you can use to quantify your benefit projections. The annual benefit of each area should be posted to the summary page so you can see your total benefit potential.

Figure 4-1
BEFORE TAX BENEFIT WORKSHEETS

Item	Example	Your Data	Annual Benefit
1. Increase Sales			
Current annual sales	$1,000,000	_____	
Projected increase	10%	_____	
Additional sales	$ 100,000	_____	
Average margin	40%	_____	
Additional gross profit	$ 40,000		_____
			Total no. 1
2. Accounts Receivable			
a. Collection period analysis			
Annual sales	$1,000.000	_____	
Daily sales	$ 2,770	_____	
(Annual sales divided by 365)			
Average or current outstanding receivables	$ 138,500	_____	
Collection period	50 days	_____	
(Outstanding A/R divided by daily sales)			
Your industry mean collection period*	42 days	_____	
Your industry high-mean collection period*	36 days	_____	
Estimated number of days your collection period may be reduced	8 days	_____	
Improved cash flow (days reduced × daily sales)	$ 22,160	_____	
Interest rate	20%	_____	
Interest saved (improved cash flow × interest rate)	$ 4,432		
			_____
			Total no. 2a

*Available through Dun and Bradstreet.

Figure 4-1
BEFORE TAX BENEFIT WORKSHEETS (Continued)

Item	Example	Your Data	Annual Benefit
b. Service charge revenue			
Net terms	30 days	_____	
No. delinquent days A/R (After projected improvement potential in collection period analysis)	12 days	_____	
	(42–30 days)		
Delinquent A/R (Delinquent days × daily sales)	$ 33,240	_____	
Finance charge %	18%	_____	
Finance charge	$ 5,983	_____	
% collectible	30%	_____	
Annual revenue	$ 1,794		
			_____
			Total no. 2b
c. Bad debt analysis			
Last year's bad debts	$ 6,000	_____	
Growth rate	20%	_____	
Projected this year's bad debts	$ 7,200	_____	
Reduction %	30%	_____	
Reduced bad debts	$ 2,400		
			_____
			Total no. 2c
d. Improved bank borrowing			
Amount borrowed on accounts receivable	$ 138,500	_____	
Reduced annual interest rate	0.5%	_____	
Interest saved	$ 692.50		
			_____
			Total no. 2d
3. Inventory			
Computing carrying cost			
Cost of capital:	20%	_____	
Opportunity cost of $:	10%	_____	
Obsolescence/Shrinkage:	2%	_____	
Taxes/Insurance:	1%	_____	
Handling/Clerical:	2%	_____	
Carrying cost†:	35%	_____	

†Use to determine annual benefit of inventory reduction in 3(a).

Figure 4-1
BEFORE TAX BENEFIT WORKSHEETS (continued)

Item	Example	Your Data	Annual Benefit
a. Inventory reduction			
Reduce by % analysis (Use either this or improved turn analysis which follows.)			
Current inventory level	$ 243,000	_____	
Carrying cost %	35%	_____	
Reduce by 10%‡			
Inventory savings	$ 24,300	_____	
Carrying cost savings	$ 8,505		_____
			Total no. 3a
Reduce by 20%‡			
Inventory savings	$ 48,600	_____	
Carrying cost savings	$ 17,010		_____
			Total no. 3a
Reduce by 30%‡			
Inventory savings	$ 72,900	_____	
Carrying cost savings	$ 25,515		_____
			Total no. 3a
Improved turn analysis (Use either this or reduce by % analysis above)			
Current inventory level	$ 243,000	_____	
Inventory turns (annual sales divided by inventory level)	4.1	_____	
Your industry mean no. turns§	6.1	_____	
Your industry high-mean no. turns§	7.6	_____	
Improved no. of turns which you project	5.0	_____	
New inventory investment (annual sales divided by improved no. turns)	$ 200,000	_____	
Inventory savings (current inventory level — new level)	$ 43,000	_____	
Carrying cost %	35%	_____	

‡Your choice
§Available through Dun and Bradstreet.

Figure 4-1
BEFORE TAX BENEFIT WORKSHEETS (continued)

Item	Example	Your Data	Annual Benefit

a. Inventory reduction (cont'd)
  Annual carrying cost
    savings
  (inventory savings $\times$
    carrying cost)
	$ 15,050		

			Total no. 3a
b. Reduced lost sales Estimated lost sales	$ 30,000	_____	
Improvement %	25%	_____	
Recaptured sales	$ 7,500	_____	
Profit margin	40%	_____	
Increased profit due to recaptured sales	$ 3,000		_____
			Total no. 3b

Item	Annual Benefit

4. Operational Productivity
  a. Direct displaceable expenses
    Equipment costs (bookkeeping machines, typewriter
      and calculator rental, maintenance, etc.)
	_____

Cost of service bureau	_____
Warehouse/plant overtime expense	_____
Outside bookkeeping expense	_____
	_____
	Total no. 4a

Item	Your Data		Annual Benefit
b. Clerical savings			
Area	Current Hours/ Year	Possible % Reduction	Hours Saved
Invoicing/Pricing	_____	50%	_____
Inventory Control	_____	50–75%	_____
Accounts Receivable	_____	50–75%	_____
Sales Analysis	_____	100%	_____

Figure 4-1
BEFORE TAX BENEFIT WORKSHEETS (continued)

Item	Your Data		Annual Benefit
Accounts Payable	_____	50%	_____
General Ledger	_____	50–75%	_____
Payroll	_____	50%	_____
Word Processing	_____	25–75%	_____
Total hours saved			_____
× cost/hour	_____		_____
	(cost/hour)		Total no. 4b

Item	Your Data	Annual Benefit
c. Avoid future hiring		
Annual growth rate	_____	
× current warehouse or plant labor costs	_____	_____
× current clerical costs	_____	_____
Total avoided costs		_____
		Total no. 4c
d. Improved efficiency		
Reduce pricing errors	_____	
Reduce picking errors	_____	
Faster reaction to price changes	_____	
Recovery of missed accounts payable discounts	_____	
Total benefits of reduced errors		_____
		Total no. 4d

Figure 4-2
SUMMARY WORKSHEET OF TOTAL BENEFITS*

	Annual Benefit
1. Increase Sales	_____
2. Accounts Receivable	
a. Improved collections	_____
b. Service charge revenue	_____
c. Reduced bad debts	_____
d. Improved bank borrowing	_____

Figure 4-2
SUMMARY WORKSHEET OF TOTAL BENEFITS* (continued)

	Annual Benefit
3. Inventory	
a. Inventory reduction/carrying cost savings (use either improved turn analysis or reduce by % analysis)	_____
b. Reduced lost sales	_____
4. Operational Productivity	
a. Direct displaceable expenses	_____
b. Clerical savings	_____
c. Avoid future hiring	_____
d. Improved efficiency	_____
Total annual benefit	_____

*Based on totals from Figure 4-1.

5

What Kind of Computer Do You Need?

At last count, there were 632 small business computers on the market. Personal, desktop, micro- and minicomputers are all advertised as being "just right for a small business." To compound the confusion, computer salespeople have a kind of radar, and the day you decide you might need a computer, it seems they're all on the phone or the doorstep. And of course, each one has precisely the right machine for you.

The purpose of this chapter is to help you sort out your alternatives. Products change so quickly—new ones come, old ones are altered—that it is virtually impossible to print anything on specific brands that will stay current. However, it is possible to classify computers according to approximate capacity and cost. This classification should give you a rough idea of the type and size of computer you need.

PERSONAL COMPUTERS

The smallest computers are called "personal computers." They are usually sold through retail computer stores and are primarily diskette based systems with one cathode ray tube. Personal computers have very small CPUs, called microprocessors, with a memory size of 16 to 64K. They may be sold without a printer, and they may cost from $500 to $5,000. Personal computers are so-named because they accommodate one user (person) at a time. They are designed to be easy to use, friendly, and personal.

Their original market was the individual computer hobbyist (usually a computer professional wanting a computer for use at home). In this environment, they are referred to as home computers and are typically used for budgeting, games, word processing, programming and self-education. These small computers may also be connected by telephone line to a large central computer containing such things as French lessons, airline schedules, and the latest press releases from the wire services. For a small monthly fee, users of personal computers can have access to the information in the large computer memory bank (paying for the amount of time they are connected).

Manufacturers of personal computers now see the business market as much larger and potentially more lucrative than the home or hobbyist market, and they are expanding the hardware and software capabilities of these small systems. In some cases, a hard disk may be attached. Some are still limited to one user systems but may be configured with sufficient memory and disk for business applications. A personal computer with a printer and appropriate for business might cost $5,000 to $15,000.

Because personal computers were originally aimed at the hobbyist who was a programmer, available software was extremely limited. Now, between the computer manufacturers and independent third party programming firms, there is a wider selection of programming available for business use: Accounting and Word Processing packages, as well as such executive aids as Financial Planning, Data Base, and Time Management programs. Because of the size of the system, the Accounting packages may be relatively unsophisticated and will generally cost $50 to $500 per module. Normally, these packages are sold off the shelf and do not include on-site training or program modifications.

MULTIUSER, BUSINESS ORIENTED MICROCOMPUTERS

Like the personal computer, the multiuser micro also uses a microprocessor CPU. The memory size is usually larger than that of a typical personal computer allowing for more sophisticated programming and multiple, simultaneous users. It may contain either floppy or hard disks, but hard disks are essential with multiple CRTs.

If you start with a single-user personal computer and grow to the point of needing a second CRT, you need to buy a new larger computer or a second personal computer. Some businesses will have several personal computers connected to each other sharing common disk files. This is called "networking." For small businesses needing two or three CRTs, it may be more economical to buy a multiuser microcomputer which will accommodate these than to buy two or three personal computers.

A business may start out with a very small computer configuration: one CRT, floppy disks, and a slow 35-character-per-second printer for under $10,000. As the business grows, a hard disk of 5 or 10 megabytes, a second screen, and a faster printer may be added. Depending on the brand and the configuration, a multiuser microcomputer will cost between $8,000 and $30,000.

A great deal of business software is available on the larger microcomputers. A typical application module such as Accounts Receivable will cost between $400 and $1,000 and will include training and documentation. Although software on a business oriented microcomputer is more costly than that developed for the personal computers, the additional function and support you receive justifies the expense.

MINICOMPUTERS

Compared with a microcomputer, a minicomputer has a more sophisticated CPU, which is faster, larger, and able to accommodate more simultaneous users. A minicomputer will always be sold with a hard disk and will have a diskette, a tape, or a removable disk for backup.

There is a certain amount of overlap between categories of computers. You may start out with a small minicomputer installation of only 64K, 10 megabytes of disk, and one CRT. This will cost more than a comparable microcomputer but because of the minicomputer's more powerful CPU technology, it will allow far more growth capacity. On a minicomputer, you can have disks holding hundreds of megabytes and you might have four to ten simultaneous users.

A typical minicomputer installation might start with 128K CPU, 25 to 50 megabytes of disk, a line printer, and three or four CRTs. This would cost $40,000 to $60,000 depending on brand, speed, and size. Because minicomputers were developed for use in business, and they have been around longer than microcomputers, more accounting software is available on these machines. Accounting packages for minicomputers are also richer in function and cost from $1,000 to $4,000 per module. Custom programming and sophisticated applications such as Inventory Management for distributors, Material Requirements Planning for manufacturers, and Estimating for contractors are usually available only on minicomputers and larger computers.

LARGER COMPUTERS

The next category up from minicomputers is commonly called supermini. Needless to say, these computers have still more capacity and are more expensive. A supermini might allow several dozen simultaneous users and have disks holding a billion characters. These computers may range in price from $80,000 to $500,000. Each application package might cost $5,000 or more, and custom programs are frequently developed. The total software cost on such a system might range from $30,000 to $100,000.

The large central computers used by *Fortune* 1000 companies are called "mainframes," and they cost millions of dollars.

SERVICE BUREAUS OR TIMESHARING?

Many businesses prefer to move into "computering" one toe at a time. As one executive said recently, "We've decided it's time to enter the twentieth century, but we're more into motor cars than space travel." For businesses not yet ready to make the commitment to buy a computer, computer services are available. You may already be using an outside service for your Payroll. Before getting your own in-house computer, you might consider letting the service bureau tackle your Accounts Receivable, Sales Analysis, and/or General Ledger. This will give you a chance to learn something about the automation of your accounting before you take the plunge.

After using a computer service bureau, most businesses rapidly decide it is preferable to have their own computer so that they can exercise some control over the operation. When you use a service bureau, you are dependent on their schedules, procedures, and formats. You can't ask for an Accounts Receivable aging report whenever you need one. You can't do an inquiry to find out if the ABC Company is over its credit limit. Unless the computer is under your roof, you cannot use it to its fullest extent. There are also delays inherent in shuffling paper and reports back and forth, correcting errors which only you seem to catch, and shuffling once again.

A timesharing service is similar to a service bureau in that the processing is done on a large central computer which is not under your roof. However, the time delays are reduced because you have in your office a terminal which is connected to the central computer by a telephone. You enter information such as customer invoice totals and checks received, and the computer keeps your Accounts Receivable figures current, produces aging reports, and so on. You are, in effect, sharing time on the computer with many other businesses, and the fee will correspond to the time you use. At certain times of the month, all the users may wish to use the computer simultaneously, and the speed with which you can enter and receive information "degrades" considerably. Timesharing is far more expensive than a service bureau, and when you use it more than 2 to 3 hours per day, it can be more economical to own a computer.

If you use any kind of computer service which is outside your control, you will be frustrated by the delays in getting reports and the inflexibility of the information provided. The report formats are theirs, not yours. On the plus side, however, a service may be less expensive than an in-house computer, and you can sign up for a short-term commitment. It's a lot like the trade-off between renting an apartment and owning a home. If you use a service, you have the flexibility of "moving out," but you do not have the flexibility of moving walls, adding on, and redecorating. It is less expensive, but you are just paying rent, not acquiring an asset. Today most computer service companies also sell in-house computers because that is what the marketplace demands. Some services will let you customize or change their programs, but the cost for this is quite high, and if you discontinue the service, you usually cannot take the programs with you or use them later on your in-house computer.

If you absolutely do not want the responsibility of an in-house computer, consider using an outside service. However, the cost of a small business computer is quite reasonable today, and these machines have been designed for the first-time user. You really do not need to be wary of having your own computer.

WHAT SIZE COMPUTER DO YOU NEED?

As a quick and dirty rule of thumb, you can use the table in Figure 5-1 to see approximately which type of computer you can cost justify. If you have a professional practice, judge computer size by the number of professionals in your firm. If you have a business, judge by annual sales. The rest of this chapter will help you estimate your business volumes and computer requirements to get a more accurate picture. The cost-justification exercise in the previous chapter should give you a more precise idea of what you can afford.

Before anyone can determine what size computer your business will

Figure 5-1
COMPUTER SIZING TABLE

Number of Professionals	Business Size (Annual Sales)	Probable Computer Type	Hardware and Software Cost	Application Complexity
1–3	Under $500,000	Personal	$ 8,000 to 15,000	Simple
2–10	$500,000 to $2,000,000	Multiuser micro	$15,000 to 30,000	Moderate
10–50	$1,000,000 to $5,000,000	Mini	$30,000 to 70,000	More complex
50+	Over $5,000,000	Large mini/ Supermini	$70,000 to 500,000	Complex

require, you need to decide what things you want to automate. Typical starter applications include:

- Accounts Payable
- General Ledger
- Accounts Receivable
- Order Processing and Billing
- Inventory Control
- Sales Analysis
- Mailing Lists
- Word Processing
- Payroll

Once you decide on the applications, you have to look at your business volumes to identify three key requirements:

1. How much disk storage do you need?
2. How many input terminals are necessary?
3. How fast a printer is required?

When you have identified your storage, input, and output requirements, you can pick the most economical computer that will meet your needs today. To plan for growth, you should estimate your volumes 2 to 3 years from now in addition to looking at today's numbers. You don't have to start out with a computer configuration big enough to handle tomorrow's volumes, but it should be expandable to meet those needs. After you have looked at your volumes, consider the following guidelines:

1. If you need more than one input terminal, you clearly cannot use a personal computer, and you will want a hard disk.
2. If you need three or more terminals, you should probably be looking at a minicomputer.
3. If you have over 2 megabytes of data to be stored, you will probably want a hard disk. While diskette systems can hold up to 5 megabytes on-line, they are substantially slower than a hard disk; and the more you store, the more aggravatingly slow they become.

The worksheets in Figures 5-2, 5-3, and 5-4 are intended to give you a rough idea of your storage, input, and output needs. Please understand that application function may vary considerably, and that one Accounts Receivable package may use a customer record size of 128 characters and another such package may use a record size of 512. The worksheets use average record sizes and input keystrokes just to give you a rough idea. The more function you want, the more these numbers will increase. Realistically, they could possibly double.

Figure 5-2
"BALLPARK" COMPUTER SIZER

Application	Your Business Volumes (A)	Record Size (B)	Disk Space (A × B)	No. of Keystrokes (C)	Monthly Keystrokes (A × C)	Print Formula (D)	Monthly Print Lines (A × D)
Accounts Receivable							
1. Total no. of customers or clients	____	× 250	= ____			× 5	= ____
2. No. of invoices per month*	____			× 125	= ____	× 1	= ____
3. × Avg. no. of months unpaid	____						
4. = No. of invoices to be stored (2 × 3)	____	×125	= ____			× 5	= ____
5. No. of checks received/month	____	× 125	= ____	× 125	= ____	× 2	= ____
Accounts Payable							
1. Total no. of vendors	____	× 250	= ____				
2. No. of invoices received per month	____	× 250	= ____	× 125	= ____	× 2	= ____
3. No. of General Ledger distributions/month	____	× 125	= ____	× 30	= ____	× 2	= ____
4. No. of checks written/month	____			× 10	= ____	× 10	= ____
General Ledger							
1. No. of General Ledger accounts	____	× 500	= ____			× 3	= ____
2. No. of journal entries/month	____	× 125	= ____	× 30	= ____	× 2	= ____
Payroll							
1. No. of employees	____	× 500	= ____				
2. No. of checks written/month	____	× 250	= ____	× 100	= ____	× 15	= ____

*Compute only if you will not be automating Billing

53

Figure 5-3
"BALLPARK" COMPUTER SIZER

Application	Your Business Volumes	Record Size	Disk Space	No. of Keystrokes	Monthly Keystrokes	Print Formula	Monthly Print Lines
Inventory							
1. No. of unique items	———	× 250	= ———			× 2	= ———
2. No. of different prices for all items	———	× 15	= ———				———
3. No. of issues/month*	———	× 125	= ———	× 30	= ———	× 2	= ———
4. No. of receipts/month	———	× 125	= ———	× 30	= ———	× 2	= ———
5. No. of adjustments/month	———	× 125	= ———	× 30	= ———	× 2	= ———
Billing							
1. No. of orders/day	———			× 2200	= ———	× 400	= ———
2. × avg. no. days open	———						
3. = No. of open orders (1. × 2.)	———	× 250	= ———				
4. × avg. no. of line items/order	———						
5. = Total line items open (3. × 4.)	———	× 125	= ———				

6. No. of line items/day (1. × 4.) _____ × 1000 = _____ × 80 = _____

7. Average no. open back orders _____ × 250 = _____ × 5 = _____

8. Total line items back ordered _____ × 125 = _____ × 5 = _____

9. No. of separate shipping addresses _____ × 125 = _____

Sales Analysis

Respond to the following items if you want 12 months
sales history for that category (double the totals for 24
months).

1. No. of customers _____ × 120 = _____ × 2 = _____

2. No. of items _____ × 120 = _____ × 2 = _____

3. No. of salesmen _____ × 120 = _____ × 2 = _____

4. No. of product classes _____ × 120 = _____ × 2 = _____

5. No. of product classes × no. of customers _____ × 150 = _____ × 2 = _____

6. No. of product classes × no. of salesmen _____ × 150 = _____ × 2 = _____

*Compute only if you will not be automating Order Processing

55

Figure 5-4
"BALLPARK" COMPUTER SIZER

Application	Your Business Volumes	Record Size	Disk Space	No. of Keystrokes	Monthly Keystrokes	Print Formula	Monthly Print Lines
Mailing Lists							
1. Total no. in mailing file	_____	× 250	= _____				
2. No. of labels/month	_____					× 5	= _____
Word Processing							
1. No. of characters to be stored on all documents	_____		= _____				
2. No. of keystrokes to be entered monthly				_____	_____		
3. Avg. no. of revisions per document	_____						
4. Avg. no. of lines produced per month	_____						
5. Total lines printed per month (3 × 4)			_____				_____
Total							
(Total Disk Space, Monthly Keystrokes, Monthly Print Lines)							

Other

If you have additional applications such as:

Bills of Material—manufacturing companies
Routings, Product Costing—manufacturing companies
Job Costing—contractors, job shops and printers
Time Accounting—law firms, CPAs

let your computer vendors tell you what size computer you need. There are too many options to attempt it here.

How to Use the Worksheets

For each application you wish to put on your computer:

1. Enter your business volumes in the first column. (If in doubt, guess high.)
2. Determine your disk requirements by multiplying your business volumes by the record size and write this in the column labeled Disk Space.
3. Determine the number of CRTs you will need. You must first calculate the number of monthly input strokes that will be keyed. To do this, multiply your business volumes by the number of keystrokes and write the answer in the Monthly Keystroke column.
4. Determine which printer you need. You must know how much printing you will be doing. Multiply your business volumes by the print formula and record the answer under Monthly Print Lines.

When you have completed the chart for each application, total up the three critical columns: Disk Space, Monthly Keystrokes, Monthly Print Lines.

ESTIMATING YOUR EQUIPMENT REQUIREMENTS

Disk Storage

You will normally keep your software and your data files on a disk. The exception to this would be if you got a personal computer or a microcomputer with only floppy disks. On these systems, each software package is on its own diskette. The data used with that package would be on a different diskette, and both would be put in the computer at the same time. But on a hard disk system, everything (software packages and data) is on one disk. The following table will help you estimate the size of disk needed.

Because software varies tremendously in complexity and size, it is difficult to give you an accurate picture of the space you will need. However, as a rule of thumb, you can use this table:

Probable Computer Type	Application Complexity	Program Storage (No. Bytes of Disk)
Desktop/Micro	Moderate	100,000/Appl.
Mini	More complex	200,000/Appl.
Large mini/ Supermini	Complex	500,000 to 1,000,000/Appl.

To determine your probable disk requirement, add the space you need for programs to the space required for your data, and double the total. Doubling allows for system software, work space for file reorganization (a periodic housekeeping chore), and some growth.

Required disk space for data _____
Required program space   _____
Total   _____
Multiply by two $\times 2$
Total disk requirement   _____

Number of CRTs

A CRT operator can do 3000 to 8000 strokes per hour, depending on experience and screen layout. To be conservative, use 5000 to determine the number of hours per day the CRT will be needed. Then you can easily see the number of screens you will need. Bear in mind that some days are busier than others, so after looking at average keystrokes per day, you may want to substitute your peak workload, or the maximum number of keystrokes you would have on your worst day.

Total number of keystrokes per month   _____
Divided by 22 = keystrokes per day   _____
Estimated maximum number of keystrokes per day   _____
Divided by 5000 = hours per day*   _____
Divided by 6 to 8 hours† = number of screens   _____

*If you are thinking about a personal computer, you can only have one CRT and you cannot use it while you are printing. To be sure you will fit on a personal computer, the CRT hours should not exceed 3 to 4 hours per day.

†You probably won't get maximum 8-hour utilization, so be conservative and use 6.

Print Requirement

Line printers (usually found on minicomputers) are rated at lines per minute. The slower dot-matrix printers (normally found on microcomputers, but also on some minicomputers) are rated at characters per second. The following formula will convert your monthly print lines to lines per minute. If you need fewer than 150 lines per minute, you can perhaps get by with a dot-matrix printer. The second part of the formula will show you what speed of dot-matrix printer you need.

Total print lines per month   _____
Divided by 22 = lines per day   _____
Estimated maximum lines per day   _____
Divided by number of hours per day = lines per
hour*   _____

Divided by 60 = lines per minute

If under 100 lines per minute, multiply by 100 and

divide by 60 to get characters per second

_____

_____

*On some microcomputers, you cannot print while entering data. If you are contemplating one of these, do not figure on printing more than 3 to 4 hours per day. Otherwise, use 6 to 7 hours per day.

SUMMARY

The purpose of this chapter was to give you a rough idea of the type of computer that will fit your business and a rougher idea of what you will need to spend. Naturally, your business will grow, and you should estimate what your needs will be 3 years from now as well as what your needs are today. Be sure the system you buy can be expanded or upgraded to handle your future requirements. The table in Figure 5-5 gives the approximate capability and cost ranges for each of the three types of small business computers.

Figure 5-5
COMPUTER CAPACITY TABLE

Type of Computer	Approximate Size Range			Hardware and Software Cost
	Disk	*CRTs*	*Printer*	
Personal	1–5 megabytes	1	Dot-matrix printer	$8,000 to 15,000
Desktop or business				
Multiuser Micro	2–20 megabytes	1–3	Dot-matrix or line printer	$15,000 to 30,000
Multiuser Minicomputer	10–100 megabytes	2–8	Line printer	$40,000 to 70,000

CHAPTER

6

What is This Thing Called Software?

Software is the key ingredient in the success or failure of your computer. Software, or programming, is the intelligence that makes a computer compute. Software makes it possible for a computer in a manufacturing company to monitor work-in-process, while the identical computer with different software might be tracking customer credit in a department store across town. It is the single most important element in your search for the right computer and, unfortunately, the most difficult and time consuming.

WHAT IS A PROGRAM?

A program is, quite simply, a set of very specific instructions which tells the computer how to perform a particular job. One program will tell the computer to print invoices, another program will be used to produce payroll checks. In other words, a unique program is developed for each specific task.

What does a program consist of? As was stated in Chapter 2, a computer performs four primary functions: it receives input, processes the information, stores it, and produces output. Our instructions to the computer, in the form of a program, pertain to these same four functions:

1. We describe the input data the computer will be working with. Is the input coming from the CRT or the disk? What is the data file name? What fields of data do we want the computer to work with?

2. We describe the calculations the computer is to perform.
3. We tell it to store the new information on the disk.
4. We describe the output. Is it a report or will the output be on the screen? How should the output be formatted?

Example: Customer Profit Report

(This is a hypothetical program and has been greatly simplified.)

1. INPUT: Read customer file; get customer name, year-to-date sales, year-to-date cost.
2. PROCESSING: Year-to-date sales minus year-to-date cost equals year-to-date profit.
3. STORE: Put year-to-date profit on the disk.
4. OUTPUT: Print customer name, year-to-date profit.

There are two primary types of computer programs: system software and application software. The example just reviewed is an application program because it applies the computer to a specific task for you. As you evaluate computer alternatives, you will be concerned primarily with application software because it determines the applicability of the computer to your business needs. Nevertheless, system software is critical to the computer's speed, function, and ease of use, so we will discuss it first. Chapter 7 is devoted to application software.

System software is integral to the operation of the computer. It is the key factor in making a computer "user friendly," or easy for the novice to operate. System software consists of three types of programs: Operating Systems, Languages, and Utilities (or Aids). This chapter provides information on each of these three types of programs. Because it gets a bit technical, you may wish to read only the first few paragraphs in each section.

OPERATING SYSTEMS

When we turn the computer on and it asks us to type in a password or today's date, we are communicating with the operating system. This is a large program which resides in the main memory, ensures the smooth operation of the computer, and communicates to the users. Its functions include:

- Validating that computer users are authorized, by checking their passwords and security codes.
- Locating the application program which each user requests and bringing it from the disk into the CPU.
- Logging internally any errors made by the computer and self-diagnosing potential hardware problems.

- Sending messages to the users when they make a mistake (such as asking for a nonexistent program).
- Checking and double checking the accuracy of what is written or read on the disk.

The operating system is usually supplied by the computer manufacturer because it is so integral to the operation of the machine. In the last few years, however, a number of specialty software houses have sprung up and developed operating systems which will function on many different computers. The smaller business computers (personal or desktop) frequently use these independent operating systems.

Because application programs are developed to run with specific operating systems, the more widely used your operating system is, the more application programs will be available to you. More important, if your operating system is a popular one, you may outgrow your first computer, but you will have a wide selection of new computers to consider without having to change your software. The most difficult aspect of learning to use a computer is working with the software. If you can change computers and keep the same software, you will drastically reduce future trauma.

When comparing computer alternatives, you should examine the operating system which each uses. Important points to consider include reliability, function, and growth.

Essentially, you need to reassure yourself regarding the following points:

1. Be sure the operating system has been around long enough to be thoroughly "debugged," that it is not some local programmer's kooky invention.
2. Be sure the operating system will support multiple, simultaneous users either if you need more than one screen today or if you will in the future.
3. Be sure that it will allow you to print while entering data (unless you are buying a personal computer).
4. Be sure you feel comfortable with its ease of use features. Is it easy to sign on to the system? Can you read the screen and understand what the computer wants you to do next? Could you come in alone in the evening and use the computer?
5. Be sure you can move to a larger computer without having to go through a horrendous conversion. Will your programs and data files move comfortably to a bigger machine? (Sometimes incompatible operating systems prevent this.)

For those of you seeking more information, here is an overview of some of the issues you need to be aware of in making a technical evaluation of an operating system.

Multiple Users

Will it handle multiple, simultaneous users? Can more than one program reside in the central processing unit at the same time? If two users are entering orders concurrently, will it prevent them from allocating the same stock to two different customers? (The feature which prevents this is called "record lock-out"; it allows only one user at a time to get at a data record. This may seem like an obscure need, but it can be important.)

Memory Management

Operating system techniques known as "virtual memory," "swapping," and "program overlays" will allow the CPU to apparently use more memory than is actually present. Programs are kept on disk and brought quickly in and out of main memory as space becomes available. With a highly developed and efficient operating system, it may be possible to run programs for four users even though the CPU is only large enough to hold two programs at once. If these techniques are used, it is vital that the system work so quickly that computer speed or response time is not degraded.

Spooling

Does the operating system allow "print spooling"? Spooling vastly improves the performance of your computer by allowing long reports to be held on disk and printed when it is convenient for you and the computer. A report can be saved and printed overnight leaving the printer free for invoices, packing slips, and important operational documents during the day. With spooling, since the report is stored on disk, you can rerun it if the paper jams in the middle. Most importantly, spooling allows you to enter data or use the computer for inquiries, while the printer is buzzing away producing a report. Without spooling or some equivalent function, the computer could be unusable to you during the printing.

Security

Does the operating system support passwords or security codes? Can you allow certain people to enter orders and others to run payroll? Can you prevent each employee from seeing any other employee's salary or the company's profits?

Indexed Files

The operating system actually works with the application program in reading and writing on the disk. It is very critical that it allow you to retrieve a specific data record so you can perform an inquiry or update an account without having to wait. Does the operating system allow direct access through either indexed files or another technique?

Self-Diagnostics

Does this operating system note its own failures, errors, and malfunctions? Are these logged internally so the maintenance people can quickly resolve problems and fix the computer?

Remote Communications

Will the operating system allow you to "talk" to your computer over a telephone line from another location? Can you communicate with your computer by using a terminal or another computer?

Other Software

Since software is built to work with a particular operating system, it is important to know what languages, utilities, and application programs are available.

If you want to act like a consultant, ask your salesman these questions regarding the operating system:

Who wrote the operating system?
How long has it been in the marketplace?
How many users are there?
Who maintains it if "bugs" occur?
What ease of use characteristics does it have?
Is it upwardly compatible to larger computers? Which computers?
Describe any conversion tasks that would have to be performed to take it
   to a larger machine.
Will it support multiple, simultaneous users? How many?
What file access techniques does it use?
Does it handle file and record lock-out to prevent simultaneous updating?
What sort of memory management will it allow?
Does it support print spooling?
Does it support simultaneous input and output?
Does it support remote communications?
Is there an extra charge for the operating system?
Is there a maintenance charge?
What languages are available with it?
What utilities are available?
Is there a library of application programs available?

LANGUAGES

We communicate in English. Machines have a language of their own. They speak an electronic language made up of electrical pulses. It is called machine language and is totally foreign to the average person. Fortunately, a few well-paid computer experts have translated machine language into something like English, allowing us to communicate with the computer. As a result, we have "programming languages," often called "high-level languages" because they can be understood by people; machine (or computer) language is considered a "low-level language." A very high-level language would be a language which is very easy for us to learn.

The most common high-level programming languages are: COBOL, BASIC, FORTRAN, RPG, and PASCAL. Each was developed for a specific purpose, and each has its own rules of grammar and syntax. For example, in RPG we tell a computer to add by saying "ADD." In FORTRAN, we would use the "+" sign. After we complete our program, it is read into the computer and translated into machine language by the appropriate language translator, or "compiler." Machine language for add might be "1011." If we used RPG, the RPG compiler translates our "ADD" into "1011." If we used FORTRAN, the FORTRAN compiler translates our "+" into "1011."

Why use one language over another? (What difference does it make anyway?)

- FORTRAN (*Formula translator*) is used for math, scientific, or problem-solving jobs. It is most likely not for you.
- COBOL (*Common business oriented language*) is the oldest language for business applications. It is an excellent, powerful language, but it is somewhat complex and often unavailable on smaller machines.
- RPG (*Report program generator*) is also excellent for business or accounting jobs and is available on many minicomputers. It is easier to learn than COBOL.
- BASIC (*Beginner's all-purpose symbolic instruction code*) is the most common language on microcomputers and is one of the easiest to learn. It is used for both business and problem-solving applications.
- PASCAL (named for the inventor of the first mechanical calculator) is a relatively new, highly efficient programming language. It is very popular with college students, so many of tomorrow's programmers know it well. It is also compatible from one computer to another, so a program written in PASCAL need not be changed when you change computers.

When you evaluate computer alternatives, you will definitely look most closely at the application software. Nevertheless, the topic of language is important to you for the following reason: Rarely will an application package fit you perfectly. Even if you are happy with it today, you may want to add to it tomorrow. If your package is written in a common, frequently used language such as one of those just described, you will have no trouble locating programmers to help you make the changes. So it pays to ask what language has been used—and consider it a plus if the language is well-known.

On the other hand, a lot of experimentation is currently under way to develop even higher level languages which will make programming easier, more efficient, and less expensive. Some computer companies are even looking at ways to let the user, who after all, knows his business best, generate his own programs by writing them virtually in English. As these tools become available, there may be compelling reasons to try a new language rather than the old tried and true. Just be sure you pinpoint who will be doing the programming and be sure they have been properly trained. Be sure the new language has a proven track record. You do *not* want to be a software pioneer. And find out how many programmers there are around who know this language. Your programmer may escape to greener pastures.

If you want more technical information, here are some additional points on languages: There are varying degrees of compatibility among languages. For example, COBOL has a national standards committee, and there is a good deal of compatibility between one company's COBOL and another's. RPG and BASIC are not regulated, and there can be a great deal of difference between various manufacturers' versions of these languages. Even two computers made by the same company may use different versions. Do not assume you can take your BASIC program to any other computer using BASIC and run it unchanged. When you buy a computer, a key issue is your ability to move to a larger computer without having to make expensive software changes. Find out which larger computers will use your operating system and language exactly as they are.

Another aspect of language selection is speed of operation. As mentioned previously, most languages compile, or translate, programs into machine language. For example, when you want to print invoices, the computer uses the translated version of that program. If you change the program to allow trade discounts, you change the original program (called the source program) and recompile it.

A more recent development is called an interpreter. You develop a program interactively under the direction of the language translator, in this case called an interpreter. It tells the programmer if he makes an obvious error and thus boosts programming efficiency. However, each time you run your program, you use the original source version, and the interpreter must be present to tell the computer what to do. (In other words, your program is not compiled once, but is translated, or interpreted, each time you run it.) As a result, interpreted programs are slower to run than compiled programs, although they can be written and changed more quickly. Programmers may like them, but they can slow down your use of the computer.

To act like a consultant, ask these questions regarding languages:

What language does this computer use?

Who developed this version, and how long has it been in the marketplace under this operating system?

Which larger computers will it run on, as is?

Will all the application packages we are looking at run without change in this language, on this machine?

How many programmers would you estimate there are in this area who are trained in it? How many on your staff?

Why was it selected for this computer?

Why was it selected for this package?

Is it an interpreter or a compiler?

UTILITIES AND AIDS

Utilities are prewritten programs produced by the equipment manufacturer. They perform commonly needed tasks so that each programmer does not have to reinvent the wheel. Utilities might perform such common functions as:

• Backing up or copying a file
• Printing or listing a file
• Sorting or resequencing the data in a file
• Deleting a temporary or out-of-date file

Since you will quite likely be using these programs, a key issue is their ease of use. One manufacturer provides a backup utility that is so complicated that only a programmer could understand how to use it. Since backup needs to be performed daily, ease of use and instruction in the use of the backup utility is critical.

Utilities have been getting fancier and more functional to allow the user to get more out of his computer without hiring a programmer. Today, the more functionally rich utilities are often referred to as user aids.

Data Base Utilities

The term "data base utility" means something far different on larger computers, but on a small computer it means a program that lets you define and create a special data file and then list or inquire into the file. Let's say that after using your computer for a year to do standard accounting, you decide to do something more personal. You want to create a data file that contains the birthdays of all of your friends and relatives. Then at the beginning of each month, you print out all of the up-coming birthdays so you can buy cards or presents. Using a data base utility, you first describe the fields in the record:

• Birthday   (month, day, year; 6 characters)
• Name   (30 characters)
• Address   (30 characters)
• City   (20 characters)
• State   (2 characters)
• Zip   (9 characters)
• Telephone number (10 characters)

Then you key in the data for each friend and family member. Next you specify what you want to print on the report and what criteria will be used to select the names printed (e.g., print all people whose birthday month is equal to the next month; print name, address, phone number, and birthday). Without a data base utility, you would need to hire a programmer to get this simple job done.

Report Writers

One of the most exciting advances in computer software within the past decade has been the development of the report writer—a tool which allows you, a nonprogrammer, to specify your own special reports.

A software package will include certain standard reports. For example, as part of an Accounts Receivable package, you will get some kind of aging report. As you start to use a computer and work with the reports, your mind will come up with a hundred ways to improve on the information you are getting. As was suggested in Chapter 4, you may want to list only customers who are over their credit limit or just those owing more than a specific dollar amount. Using a Report Writer, you can feed these variables to the computer and get your uniquely described report. Examples 1 and 2 illustrate how easy it is to use a Report Writer:

Example 1

What items should be returned to the vendor because surplus stock exists? What is the total value of this stock?

Your Instructions:

```
READ            ITEM FILE

SELECT          QTY ON HAND        >    MAXIMUM
OR,             DATE LAST SALE      <    6/1/82
OR,             NO. MONTHS SUPPLY   >    6
TITLE           OVERSTOCK REPORT
PRINT           VENDOR #
                ITEM #
                DESCRIPTION
                QTY ON HAND
                MAX
                DATE LAST SALE
                YTD SALES
                AVG. MO. SALES
                NO. MOS. SUPPLY
                UNIT COST
TOTAL           ON HAND VALUE
```

Generate This Report:

OVERSTOCK REPORT										12/1/82
VENDOR #	ITEM #	DESCRIPTION	QTY ON HAND	MAX	DATE LAST SALE	YTD SALES	AVG. MO. SALES	NO. MOS. SUPPLY	UNIT COST	ON HAND VALUE
1601	178956	DLX 3-hole Punch	78	60	3/7/80	31	8	9.7	$12.35	$ 963.30
	18621	Adding Machine	168	150	4/6/80	17	5.4	31	$56.50	$ 9,492.00
								TOTAL		$10,455.30

Example 2

Which customers have a delinquent balance larger than $2,500 and over 90 days old?

Your instructions:

READ	CUSTOMER FILE	
SELECT	OVER 90	> $2,500.00
SORT	OVER 90-DESCENDING	
TITLE	OVER 90 REPORT	
PRINT	CUSTOMER NAME	
	CONTACT NAME	
	TEL. NO.	
	TOT. DUE	
	CURRENT	
	OVER 30	
	OVER 60	
	OVER 90	

Generate This Report:

OVER 90 REPORT							
CUSTOMER NAME	CONTACT NAME	TEL. NO.	TOT. DUE	CURRENT	OVER 30	OVER 60	OVER 90
SMITH & CO.	JIM	(213) 921-6141	6,886	1,086	1,840	940	3.020
BARNABY INTL.	CANDY	(714) 871-6042	5,025	1,070	945	870	2,140

Queries

Frequently, a Report Writer will also allow you to perform inquiries into a data file. If so, the utility is often called a Query and Report Writer. The query function allows you to specify a particular condition that you are seeking and receive the answer on the screen. You might want to see the status of a particular customer or find out which customers are over their credit limits. Examples 3 and 4 illustrate how you might use the query function.

Example 3

The status of a particular customer . . .

Your Instructions:

```
READ          CUSTOMER FILE
SELECT        CUSTOMER NO.        =        134
DISPLAY       CUSTOMER NO.
              CUSTOMER NAME
              YTD SALES
              TOTAL DUE
              CURRENT
              OVER 30
              OVER 60
              OVER 90
```

Generate This Screen:

```
CUSTOMER NO.:              134
CUSTOMER NAME:            ASSOCIATED MARINE
YTD SALES:               $11,870.00
TOTAL DUE:                 1,870.00
CURRENT:                   1,150.00
OVER 30:                     615.00
OVER 60:                     105.00
OVER 90:                       0.00
```

Example 4

Search for a specific condition:
What back orders exist for part #106-AC?

Your Instructions:

```
READ        ORDER FILE
SELECT      PART NO.           =      106-AC
            ORDER STATUS       =      B.O.
            PART NO.
DISPLAY     CUSTOMER NO.
            CUSTOMER NAME
            ORDER NO.
            ORDER DATE
            QTY ON ORDER
```

Generate This Screen:

```
        PART NO.:        106-AC
   CUSTOMER NO.:         1759
 CUSTOMER NAME:         APPLIED ELECTRONICS
      ORDER NO.:         18069
    ORDER DATE:         3-19-80
  QTY ON ORDER:         550
```

7

What about Application Software?

Application programs, as stated in the previous chapter, are the key ingredient in making sure the computer meets your needs. They "apply" the computer to your business and are, therefore, usually purchased with the computer. For small businesses, the most common applications are

- Accounts Receivable
- Inventory Control
- Order Processing and Billing
- Sales Analysis
- Accounts Payable
- General Ledger
- Mailing Lists
- Payroll
- Word Processing
- Financial Planning

In addition to these applications, specialty application packages exist for insurance companies, CPAs, doctors, lawyers, manufacturers, job shops, distributors, retailers, property management companies, and so on. This chapter will explain techniques for evaluating and acquiring application software.

There are two ways in which you can get your computer to run the applications you need. You can buy a prewritten ("canned") software package, or you can hire a programmer and develop your own. Naturally, developing your own is more expensive and also fraught with all the frustrations and demands on your time you would experience if you built your own home. On the other hand, if you move into a tract house, it may be easier and less expensive, and you may be able to move in sooner, but something is going to displease you. Most companies, however, favor the package approach. A package can be modified slightly to tailor it more to your liking, but don't expect to make major changes and still retain the benefits of the package approach: economy and timeliness. If you are in the market for an economical microcomputer, you will definitely want off-the-shelf packages.

The software dilemma for most businesses boils down to: which package fits best, and if you need changes, which company do you trust to modify it at the best price, with the fewest problems, in the shortest period of time? Also at issue are support services such as training, documentation, installation planning, and so on, the working relationship your people will have with the software personnel, and, of course, the cost. Software is so important that all experts agree you should select your software package before you choose your computer.

EVALUATING PACKAGE FIT AND FUNCTIONS

Application functions vary. It is easy to be impressed with a glamorous package, rich in function, and loaded with exotic reports which you may not even need. But which package best fits your business? At the risk of sounding obvious, you need to begin the evaluation with a thorough understanding of your own business, its operations, problems, and priorities.

Small businesses often have one of three major problems in finding appropriate software:

1. They do not take the time to analyze and prioritize their needs.
2. They do an inadequate job of communicating their needs to computer vendors.
3. They assume that because they have verbally explained their needs to the computer salesman the software will do the job. (The salesman may not be totally aware of the functions in his package.)

The result of any of these problems is inadequate package fit.

You are the buyer. The burden is on you to "buy smart." To ensure that you buy the right software, you must do two things after you have determined your requirements and priorities:

1. Review each package in enough detail to ensure it fits.
2. List your requirements in specific detail in the contract with your software vendor, if modifications are necessary.

HOW DO YOU ANALYZE YOUR SOFTWARE NEEDS?

The first place to start is with the heart of your business operation. For manufacturers and distributors, the most difficult application areas to fit are Order Processing, Billing, and Inventory. Quantity pricing, discounts, unit of measure conversions, back order policy, and costing techniques will vary tremendously from one business to the next. Furthermore, these are among the most difficult and complex things to program. They can be a nightmare to modify if they don't fit properly. All too often, businesses gloss over their order processing procedures and assume a package will fit. A year later, they throw out the computer because after months of effort the package could not be modified to do pricing properly.

For other types of firms, the key applications are also those which relate to the day to day operation of the business. For printers, job shops, and contractors, it's Job Costing and Estimating. For lawyers and CPAs, it's Billing and Time Accounting. Please be sure you thoroughly understand and document all the complexities and exceptions of your operation and explain these in painstaking detail to all computer vendors you are considering. Be sure you distinguish the way you think things are done, from the way you hope it is done, from the way it is done!

After you have examined the operational heart of your business, look at those applications which you expect to generate the highest return for your business. After referring to Chapter 4, decide which application areas will generate the greatest benefit. What special reports do you believe would most help you to achieve that benefit? When you look at the various packages, are these reports included? If not, is the data you want on the report available in the data files?

One of the easiest package modifications is adding a report when the required data is available. Let's assume you want a customer year-end profit report. If your customer file contains sales and profit figures for the past 12 months, you can use a Report Writer to print a profit ranking report. However, if the package is programmed only to accumulate sales, without cost or profit figures, you are looking at a major and very traumatic programming change. The data file needs to be altered to hold additional data, and the invoicing package needs to be changed to post not only sales but also cost of sales to the customer master record. In other words, if the data is in the master record, it is easy to get it printed. If it's not there, forget it. So when you evaluate a package, first look at the reports. If the report you want is not there, look at the data file structure to see if it can be obtained. Or ask your computer sales rep to do this for you.

One way to improve the likelihood of a close application fit is to buy a package that either was written for someone in your industry or was used by someone with a similar business. There is no guarantee that they do business exactly as you do, so the package still requires examination.

Do not expect a perfect fit of any application package. Even custom programs often sacrifice some desired function for economy. But be sure the package fits the most critical functional areas. So begin by prioritizing those things which must fit, those things which would be nice, and so on. More information to assist you with this is included in Appendix B and in Chapter 10.

If you are buying a microcomputer, you will be looking at application packages which are relatively unsophisticated. Be prepared to sacrifice some items on your "want list." You should decide which one or two applications are the most important. For example, if they are Word Processing and Inventory Control, look for the microcomputer with the best versions of these packages which also has the other applications you need. You will pretty much have to accept the other applications (e.g., Accounts Receivable) as they are. If you are really fussy on every single application, you will never find a computer.

In addition to function, an important aspect of package selection is ease of use. Some packages are so complicated that they are traumatic for the average user, so be sure to see a demonstration.

ACQUIRING SOFTWARE

Application packages are available from many sources and with varying degrees of support. Considering the source can be as important, or more important, than looking at application fit and function.

Looking for the right software is usually an integral aspect of looking for the right computer. Most businesses acquire both from the same source— one stop shopping. A company which sells and supports both hardware and software is referred to as a "single source vendor." They will usually provide documentation, training, program modification, hardware maintenance, and all the support services you need to get a computer up and running. Another term for this is "turnkey installation." With a single source vendor, you have only one number to call for any problem which should arise. Because they are getting revenue from both hardware and software sales, they have good financial incentive to perform for you—especially before they have been fully paid.

In some cases, however, an independent, or third party, programming firm has the best software for your needs. If you elect to buy their package, they will direct you to a source for the hardware. In theory, if you have computer problems later, you could experience some finger pointing between the hardware and software vendors. Although this can occur, it is minimized if the two vendors have an established working relationship and the software has a proven track record. Incidentally, some so-called single source vendors who sell hardware and software actually use an independent source for hardware maintenance. This, too, can lead to the same type of finger pointing.

If you should need custom programming or package modifications, you are safest if you buy from a single source vendor who is willing to do custom programming. Because you are buying both hardware and software, you have maximum financial leverage to ensure that the custom programming is completed before you accept the computer. If you buy hardware from A and software from B, you may have to pay A for the computer before B has finished the programs. While you have some clout with the software company and can withhold final payment until the programs are complete, there have been a few incidents of programmers walking away from final payment rather than complete what has turned out to be a sticky job.

On the other hand, in many cases independent programmers perform excellent work at very economical prices. They are entrepreneurs, unsaddled with large overhead, often very eager to do a superior job and establish or maintain a top-notch reputation. If you are considering an independent programming firm, the deciding factors should be their reputation for quality and timely work and their knowledge of your industry.

Another approach is to buy a program developed by another business in your industry. This package might fit you like a glove, but please be wary, particularly if the other business is in another state. The package may be working fine for them, but who in your home town knows how to work with it? Who will modify it if your sales tax is changed? Who will make the changes if you have a different discounting system? Who will program the additional reports you will inevitably dream up? Who will come out to help your operator learn to use it in the first place and get out of a jam in the second place? Who will sell you the proper hardware to run it on, and will that be a good buy? The availability of support can be almost as important as the fit and quality of the package. Packages developed by friends are rarely documented as clearly and thoroughly as packages from reliable programming firms. This makes it very difficult to resolve operational problems without assistance.

Whether you acquire the software from a hardware vendor or an independent source, be sure the price of the package includes all the training, documentation, and support you will need. (Specific negotiations are discussed in Chapter 13.) You should be looking for a combination of good package fit and solid support services.

8

Computer Disasters Are Not for You

Let's face it, the computer industry has a bad name. People love to tell about their favorite computer screw up. It's human against machine and, clearly, a human wins a human's sympathy vote. Is it a bum rap? Or, are the nightmarish machine malfunctions all true? And if the disaster stories are true, have all the malfunctions really been the machine's fault?

If you mow off your toe, is it the lawnmower's fault or yours? Computers, like all tools, have no will of their own. They will do precisely what you tell them. But because computers are more complex and powerful than most other tools, they are harder to control and use properly—and the problems can be disastrous. One new computer user, upon surveying an entire run of customer statements in which the balance due accumulated from one statement to the next (the last customer owed the sum of all the others), said mournfully, "Old Mary at her worst never made a mistake like this."

Computer disasters do happen, but they are generally predictable and avoidable—particularly if the computer is used for applications which have been performed before. In the sixties, when computers were first used extensively by business, there were no application packages. The industry was populated by programmers who were hired out of technical schools and told to "put the company on the computer." It is small wonder that the programs they designed sometimes failed to meet the requirements of the real world. Inventory systems didn't allow for free samples or returned merchandise. Accounts Receivable programs didn't allow for a service charge that might never be paid and kept sending delinquency notices for $0.17, and so on.

Today the computer industry has matured. Hardware is cheaper and far more reliable. Many programmers have accounting degrees or at least lots of direct business experience. The quality of programming has vastly improved and most businesses buy proven packages—at least to start. However, the industry still has problems. And, most of the problems occur with software, particularly when it is modified or customized.

Here is today's dilemma in a nutshell:

1. Virtually every computer installed needs some custom programming, or the business needs to adjust its methods around the packaged program. (Rarely does a package fit perfectly.)
2. Existing programming techniques are still in the Dark Ages. There have not been programming advancements comparable to hardware breakthroughs, and programming changes are still time-consuming, cumbersome, expensive, and fraught with opportunity for error.
3. There aren't enough programmers to go around.
4. Today's business executive rarely takes the time in advance to look closely at the package he is getting to be sure it fits properly—so there are always more changes required than have been anticipated.
5. The computer salesman spends even less time trying to see if his package fits the customer, because he sure doesn't want to find out that it doesn't! (His programmer will clean up the mess.)

Are you getting the picture? The result of this is that many computer users feel that they are being shortchanged. They must either live with a program that is not quite right or endure the trauma of custom programming. When programmers are involved, there are almost always surprises: extra unanticipated programming charges, delays, and problems. Things never happen as quickly as promised because virtually all programmers are spread too thin. Half the time, business owners can't even get hold of their programmer by phone if they have a question or problem. It is not a dishonorable industry, but it is in a state of awkward growth and development.

Does this mean you shouldn't get a computer? Absolutely not! If you want the benefits of automation, and they are considerable, and you are willing to invest some time to get them, you can minimize the potential for disaster. If you are to achieve computer success, you need, (1) a package that fits as closely as possible, and (2) an arrangement with your computer vendor which will improve the likelihood that you receive your fair share of support. How do you achieve these two things? First, let's review some real life computer horror stories.

CASE NUMBER 1: THE GLOSSY ESTIMATE

A temporary-help employment agency bought a computer to keep track of the hours worked by each employee for each client, to do the billing, and to write the payroll checks. It sounded simple to the computer salesman who glossed over the details with his programmer. The programmer never met the customer until after the sale. The customer was thrilled with the salesman's programming estimate of $6,000, when all the other vendors he was considering were quoting $12,000 to $15,000. It was too good to be true and, in fact, it wasn't true. Once the deal was signed and the downpayment paid, the programmer took his first close look at the job. He then had the pleasure of telling the customer it would really cost $18,000.

MORAL:

1. Be suspicious of low bids.
2. Always meet the person who is actually going to do the work.
3. Be sure you thoroughly explain what you want. Never assume the bidders know.
4. Get a thorough description in writing of what the bidders propose to do.

CASE NUMBER 2: THE VANISHING COMPLETION DATE

A cheese distributor bought a computer to do Order Processing, Billing, and Inventory. He found an independent programmer who had once installed Billing for a plumbing distributor and hired him to develop all of his applications. The estimate was $17,000 and 6 months of work. The project was still unfinished 18 months and $43,000 later. The computer operator had a minor nervous breakdown over the problems. The owner of the business lost an additional $72,000 in computer rental charges and an estimated $50,000 in sales because of order entry mistakes. The deeper into the programming, the more the business owner was afraid to fire the programmer. He didn't want to walk away from his investment, and he knew no programmer would be able to unscramble another's undocumented disaster.

MORAL:

1. Try to find a package which fits as closely as possible or a programmer who knows your business.
2. Review the design or plan of all the custom programs in their early stages to be sure they fit.
3. Maintain and monitor a schedule. It should be broken down into many measurable projects and not just one unmanageable marshmallow.
4. Trust your instincts. If the schedule keeps slipping and you lose confidence in your programmer, don't be afraid to cut your losses. (But don't fire him on the first screw up; there will be mistakes.)

CASE NUMBER 3: THE PERFECT PACKAGE

An office supply distributor wanted a computer to free himself from tedious overwork. He needed more control over his business and more time to plan and to develop strategy. Obviously, he had very little time to dig into the computer decision and neither did any of his people. He thought it would be a waste of money to hire a consultant, so he called computer companies listed in the phone book and asked, "Do you have a package for office supply distributors?" Guess what they all answered? (Hey, Harold, I've got a live one here. Brush off the hardgoods distributor's proposal and type 'office supply' on the front.") The distributor really wanted it to be easy. He didn't want to talk to lots of computer salesmen. "After all, one computer is as good as another." Oh, he did his homework—he read all three proposals, he looked through the sample reports, and he phoned three references for each company. None of the references were in his industry, but what difference did that make? Everything looked good, so he bought the least expensive package. Six months later, he found out the "perfect package" wouldn't handle his pricing. He was astonished. Any package made for his industry ought to handle contract pricing! He was also poorer—he had paid $7,000 to fix the problem. What choice did he have? He had already bought the computer.

MORAL:

1. There is no easy way out. You have to examine the package in detail to be sure it fits. Or have it stated in the contract that the computer will be made to perform specific functions and list them all.
2. Try to talk to references in *your* industry.

CASE NUMBER 4: AND NARY A TRACE WAS LEFT

A marine distributor hired an independent programmer to do his Order Processing, Billing, Inventory, and so on. The programming went fairly smoothly and was completed only 3 months behind schedule. (This is actually pretty good—nothing is ever on schedule.) The programmer zoomed in, gave a demonstration, left a yellow pad with some hand scribbled instructions on it, collected his check, and went off on vacation. To say that the distributor had operational difficulties, many questions, and a heavy case of hysteria, would be an understatement. There had been no training, there were no clear written instructions, and everyone was confused and frightened. When the programmer returned, he did do some additional training, but never completed the promised documentation. Since he had been paid, he was more interested in new customers and was hard to reach even by phone. He told the distributor that, for a monthly retainer, he would give him additional assistance. We cannot print what the distributor replied. They now hate each other.

MORAL:

1. Complete programming services include training and documentation. These should be scheduled, and complete payment should not be made until they are done.
2. Independent programmers do live on a shoestring. If you need something which you did not include in the original contract, you may have to pay more than anticipated. Or perhaps you can help the programmer by being a reference. Try to work out a mutually beneficial arrangement.

CASE NUMBER 5: WHY BOTHER WITH A DEMO?

A distributor of imported shoes bought a standard Order Processing package from a highly reliable major computer company. He invested the time to review it carefully and examined all of the reports and data file contents. He was elated with his decision and couldn't wait to get the package. He didn't bother to see a demonstration of the package because he trusted the vendor implicitly. Not until he received the computer and tested the software did he realize that it had been developed for a company that only back ordered 5 to 15 percent of the items ordered. In his industry, 40 to 60 percent of the items ordered had to be back ordered. Because the back order routines were so cumbersome, it took his computer 2 hours at the end of each day to match new inventory receipts to existing back orders. During this time, nothing else could be done on the machine. He ended up developing an entirely new software system to handle his job properly.

MORAL:

1. Review the operational characteristics of a package as well as the key reports—particularly in areas where you know you have unusual problems or requirements.
2. Go visit other users and see a live demonstration of the package. Ask them what they like and don't like. This problem should have come out *before* the purchase.

CASE NUMBER 6: THE SPEARED PIONEER

A distributor of imported gift items enjoyed being the first with any new item. He decided to be the first in his community (which was Los Angeles!) to buy the newest model of a fairly well known computer manufacturer. It was so new that the local sales office didn't even have a demonstrator. No one had ever seen one, but the brochures were lovely, and the price was great. The payment terms were simple: cash on delivery. After the distributor had it for 7 months the computer company got it working. It seems there were a few "design" errors in the disk drive: data entered could never be found again.

MORAL:

1. The pioneer is the one with the spear in his back.

CASE NUMBER 7: MAD FINGERS MADELEINE

A distributor of janitorial supplies got a computer to do all of the usual distribution applications. They spent 2 months keying in customer master records and sales history. At first they backed up their files daily, but this became a bore, and since they never seemed to need it, they gradually stopped. They finally had all of the historic data captured and were ready to go live with Accounts Receivable. Madeleine, the operator, spent all weekend typing in current accounts receivable balances so they could start live operations on Monday. Unfortunately, Madeleine got tired and a bit confused. She posted some of the balances twice and didn't know how to reverse the entries. She then tried to delete these customers and reenter the data correctly, but she accidentally deleted the entire file. After her boss was told about this on Monday, he reinstituted backup.

MORAL:

1. Do backup daily.
2. Don't let a frightened new operator spend the weekend alone performing a critical conversion. Her boss should have been there, and the programmer should have at least been available by phone.

CASE NUMBER 8: HARRY GOT EVEN

An industrial supply distributor got a computer to modernize operations. It was made clear to all employees that they should learn to use the new computer or find another job. Poor Harry had done all inventory accounting and purchasing for 27 years. He was positive he was going to be replaced by the computer—if the computer ever got up and running. He tried to show interest and asked the young, outside programmer to show him a little bit about the computer. The programmer never asked him for his advice on the inventory program. Harry finally figured out a way to save his job: change some of the data on the disk every day so no one would trust the computer. Unfortunately, Harry was found out and fired. But Harry had learned enough about computer operations to erase the whole disk which, of course, he did on the way out.

MORAL:

1. Involve your people in the whole process of selecting a computer. Don't let them feel their jobs are in jeopardy. Ask for their recommendations in their areas of expertise.
2. If you are forced to fire someone, get him out the door quickly and maintain security around the computer.

CASE NUMBER 9: THE MISSING PACKAGE

A contractor bought a computer from a new computer company. They didn't have their software "completely working," so they were unable to demonstrate it, but they showed him all the reports and functions they had planned. The contractor liked the salesman and knew the programmers were experienced, so he ordered the computer. Unfortunately, two years later, the package still wasn't "completely finished." During that time, the executive tried every pressure tactic he could think of, but nothing helped. The computer company genuinely wanted to deliver, but they were simply unable to meet their commitments. They finally went out of business.

MORAL:

1. No matter how much you like and trust the people, demand to see concrete evidence of their product—a working demonstration and live references.

CONCLUSION

How do you achieve computer success? There is a consistent thread running through each of these stories. Problems occurred because management was not sufficiently involved. The owners of these businesses did not want to spend sufficient time to properly:

- Plan for the computer by setting objectives and requirements
- Evaluate computer alternatives thoroughly to select the best package
- Negotiate for the best possible support commitment and contractual arrangement
- Manage and review the progress of the installation tasks
- Involve employees and create enthusiasm

There is no escaping it. Where management gets involved, computer disasters rarely happen.

PART

TWO

How to Select the Right Computer

CHAPTER

9

Selecting Your First Computer

After reading this far, you should have the following things clearly in mind:

- What hardware and software are.
- What general benefits you can expect from a computer.
- Approximately how much money you are going to have to spend.
- That it is going to require a considerable amount of your time and energy to make the whole thing happen successfully.

At this point, you probably have an idea of whether you want a computer. The rest of this book is devoted to the selection and acquisition process. This chapter will give you an overview of the process.

Selecting the right computer for your business really involves four integrated decisions:

1. Choosing a software package that fits your business.
2. Selecting a computer that will handle your business volumes.
3. Choosing a vendor whose support services and commitment meet your expectations.
4. Selecting an overall program which fits your pocketbook.

DETERMINING THE BUDGET AND SCOPE OF THE PROJECT

When working with a client, a consultant will usually start by determining what applications they want to put on the computer, how large their volumes are, and how much they want to spend on the whole project. If you want to do nine applications and can spend only $20,000, some expectations need to be adjusted. If you don't begin with some idea of your spending limitation, you can waste a lot of time looking at exotic and expensive alternatives.

On the other hand, if a $2 million company wants to spend only $20,000, this is equally unrealistic. A cost-justification exercise (as shown in Chapter 4) identifying the dollar benefits of automation should illustrate that they can afford more. As a rule of thumb, most businesses can afford to spend 2 to 4 percent of their annual gross sales on a computer package (hardware, software, and incidental expenses). Chapter 4 should help you determine the dollar benefit of using a computer. Chapter 5 will give you an idea of what you will need to spend. Between the two, you can probably come up with a realistic budget.

DETERMINING YOUR APPLICATION REQUIREMENTS

After you know what your spending limitation is, it pays to give more detailed thought to what you want to automate and why. What areas of the business do you want to improve? In what ways can they be improved? What specific goals do you have? What information will help you achieve these goals? Before you begin a serious search for a computer, it is wise to have a list of:

• Application Priorities
• Specific functions and reports for each application

Chapters 3 and 10 should help you with this.

WHERE TO BUY A COMPUTER

Once you have identified your approximate budget and listed your application priorities you can begin the search for THE computer. At this point you can waste a lot of time and energy looking for the right computer in the wrong place. Computers are sold through a variety of sales organizations: (1) manufacturers, (2) independent sales organizations (ISOs), and (3) retail computer stores and department stores. It is important to understand the characteristics of each of these to know where your computer may be found.

A few of the larger computer manufacturers have their own direct sales force. These include IBM, Burroughs, NCR, and Wang. They sell their own computers and a limited selection of application programs. They will provide hardware maintenance, installation advice and guidance, and training on their application packages. If you need program modifications or additional software, they will generally lead you to an independent or third party program-mer. Usually, the computers sold by a direct (and expensive) salesforce will tend to be the larger (and expensive) minicomputers.

Other computer manufacturers choose to sell their products through inde-pendent sales organizations (ISOs) which may be referred to as original equip-ment manufacturers (OEMs), dealers, distributors, or systems houses. Com-puters sold this way include those manufactured by Digital Equipment Corporation (DEC), Data General, Hewlett Packard, and Texas Instruments. These independent companies normally provide turnkey installations. They order the hardware for you, sell you the application packages, and do all of the programming modifications and training. Terms such as authorized dealer or master distributor usually mean that the firm also provides hard-ware maintenance. If you want a true single source vendor, look for a com-pany which sells and supports both hardware and software. ISOs sell every-thing from the larger microcomputers to superminis, but generally they do not sell personal computers.

Personal computers and some multiuser microcomputers are sold almost exclusively through retail computer stores or department stores. The profit on these sales is simply not great enough for a sales rep to call on you per-sonally. They will not survey your business and tell you what you need. The burden is on you to identify your needs, go to the store, and select the best system. The stores sell off-the-shelf software which may be limited in func-tion. If you are buying a personal computer, the application packages will include an instruction manual. Other than a demonstration in the store, you will probably receive no in-person training. If you buy a multiuser microcom-puter with more sophisticated and expensive programming, you may receive some on-site training. The more you spend, the more you get, and training may be negotiable.

Two types of hardware maintenance are usually offered. For a monthly fee of approximately 1 percent of the hardware cost, you take the computer into the store to be fixed. For about 1.5 percent of the hardware cost, a repairman will come to your office. Most stores do not offer programming services because they simply do not have the staff, although they may refer you to an independent programmer. Because of the tremendous economies of the store approach, more small computers will be sold this way and the variety of services offered by the more enterprising stores is bound to increase.

WHERE SHOULD YOU BE LOOKING?

If your budget is under $20,000 for hardware and software, you are a candi-date for a micro. In this case, your best bet is to go to a computer store (or several stores), see some demonstrations, and buy the package that most closely matches your needs. Plan on automating only those applications which will fit on a small computer. You may want to do Word Processing, Mailing Lists, Accounts Payable, General Ledger, Billing, Inventory, Accounts Receivable and so on. But if your budget calls for a personal computer with only one input screen, you may not be able to automate all these operations. You will need to adjust your expectations and prioritize what you want. Look for a small microcomputer which can later be expanded to a hard disk and multiple CRTs when your budget also expands. If you buy a microcomputer from a computer store, do not expect the application packages to be tailored to your business. While some stores do offer programming services or pass on the names of independent programmers, these services are expensive and will blow your limited budget. Do not expect to buy a sophisticated Order Processing or Inventory Control package. These applications are too complete to be sold "off the shelf" without training or modifications.

Do not plan on the salesperson's helping you extensively in an in-depth analysis of your application needs. Each store usually has one or two people who are experienced in the business use of computers and several other salespeople who are not. They may know the details of one or two application packages they are selling, but may not have a comprehensive view of what is on the market. They may not have the time or experience to help you delve into a long list of your requirements to be sure a package fits you, or be able to help you compare and contrast alternative packages.

You are more likely, however, to encounter a salesperson with strong business and computer expertise in a store that sells only computers than in a store carrying many diverse products. In any case, the burden will be on you to make sure you are buying the best package. Be sure you put together a checklist of your needs before you begin the search. If the checklist is short, simple, and specific, and you go to a computer store which specializes in selling business oriented micros, you can probably find a salesman who can help you identify the best one or two packages. The chapters on laying out your software needs, preparing a request for proposal (RFP), and evaluating vendors will help you prepare a good checklist.

If your budget is higher, and especially if it is above $30,000, you can expect more service in both the selection and implementation of the computer. You can expect a sales representative to call on you, compare your requirements to his application packages, and write a proposal. For this kind of treatment, you would go to either an independent sales organization (an OEM, Systems House, or Master Distributor), or one of the manufacturers which sells directly to the end user. The more you are willing to spend, the more personal service you will receive. The table in Figure 9-1 illustrates the products and support you can expect from the various types of computer vendors.

Figure 9-1
SUPPORT COMPARISON OF COMPUTER VENDORS

Service or Product Provided	Computer Vendors			
	Manufacturers with Direct Sales Force	Authorized or Master Distributors	OEMs or Systems Houses	Computer Stores
Analysis of your needs	yes	yes	yes	no
Written proposal	yes	yes	yes	no
Hardware sale	yes	yes	yes	yes
System software	yes	yes	yes	yes
Application package	sometimes	yes	yes	yes
Programming modifications	usually not	yes	yes	no
Application training	sometimes	yes	yes	sometimes
Ongoing support	sometimes	yes	yes	no
Hardware maintenance	yes	yes	sometimes	sometimes
Financing (lease or rent)	yes	sometimes	usually not	sometimes

PREPARING TO TALK TO COMPUTER VENDORS

Whether you are planning to go to a computer store or ask a salesman to call on you, you should begin with a written list of your application requirements. Chapter 10 will help you get these down on paper.

10

Laying Out Your Software Needs

Many people select software packages (and thus the computer as well) the way that children pick out toys. They gravitate to the snazziest, most eye-catching selection, not to the products that are the most useful and well-made. In fact, computer companies will deliberately demonstrate the parts of an application package which have the most "sex appeal" because they know this will sell the package. A common expression in the industry is, "The sizzle sells the steak." Often, buyers do not know what they need in the first place and do not want to take the time to examine the package in the second place. They are content to be "sold," to see just those flashy things the salesperson chooses to show them. In the end, all they can do is select according to sizzle.

An Order Processing package with sizzle will cause the screen to blink at you if you try to enter an order for a customer who is over his credit limit. Another package might simply hold the order and print a report informing you that the customer is over his limit. This is a less exciting approach to the problem but, in fact, a report which goes to management and lists all of the problem accounts might be more useful than a screen blinking at an operator who has no authority to resolve the situation. The real key is that the package you select meet your functional needs. If you have a problem with long overdue delinquent balances, you undoubtedly want a package which addresses the problem of delinquent customers who continue to order more. You also need to be sure the package fills your other needs and handles your pricing, discounting, unit of measure conversions, and so on.

Do not be overly swayed by snazzy things such an inquiry screens. They are among the easiest things to program, and you can often do them with a Query and Report Writer; however, the accounting logic of a package is central and essential to the package and virtually impossible to change.

Sizzle might well be the final deciding point in choosing one package over another. But if you begin a comparison with a knowledge of the specific functions you need, you have a far better chance of ensuring that your selection will do the job. As you know, application software is the most critical element in your computer buying decision. It will either make or break the entire project. The wrong software will demoralize you and everyone who touches the computer. The right software will make your healthy business run even more successfully.

Therefore, please start your search for a computer with a concrete list of your application needs. If you know what you want, it will take you longer to make a selection, but you will save oceans of time in the long run because you will make the right selection. The tricky part is knowing what you want.

IDENTIFYING APPLICATION PRIORITIES

The computer needs to handle those aspects of your business which are working well for you, those things which you do not want to change, and those new functions which your current system cannot handle. It must help you achieve your business goals by providing important information you are not able to get today.

The surest way of defining your software needs is a top-down approach where you start with company goals and work down to the information and procedures needed at all levels to achieve those goals. You can work alone on this hefty project, or you can involve your top employees in the process. It is an excellent idea to hold a planning or brainstorming session with key employees before you finalize your application needs.

THE PLANNING SESSION

The purpose of the planning session is to involve your employees in the process of making your business more successful. You are soliciting their ideas, support, and commitment to help your business become more profitable and efficient.

At the beginning of the meeting, you should present specific goals for your company. They need to be measurable so you can evaluate your progress in the future.

Examples of Specific, Measurable Goals:

- Increase sales by 30 percent per year without adding salesmen.
- Shorten collection period from 53 to 46 days within 6 months.

- Improve inventory turns from 5.2 per year to 6.0 within 1 year.
- Improve customer service by reducing stockouts from 15 percent to 10 percent.

Next, explain the purpose of the planning session—to get employees' ideas—and encourage them to contribute. Ask the group to describe all the problems they see with the current operation of the company. These problems should then be expressed in clear complete sentences and written on flip charts. At least 2 hours should be spent on problem definition, and all functional areas of the business should be covered. You need to be unintimidating—so either keep quiet or leave the room! (You may want to consider appointing someone else to lead this portion of the meeting.)

Examples of Problems Which Impact Company Goals and Smooth Operations:

- The order processing paperwork is so cumbersome that we cannot ship and invoice the same day.
- Stockouts are increasing in all products made by the ABC Company.
- The price list is so hard to read that pricing errors are frequent.
- It takes 2 weeks after month end to get out statements.
- The salesmen can't get current information on stock availability.

Next, ask employees for their creative suggestions on how to handle these problems in order to meet the company's goals. Financial and other constraints should be given to avoid wild "blue sky" solutions. It may be necessary to divide into groups if the problems are too numerous. Ask them to outline what additional information would help them work more effectively and how they think a computer could assist them in day to day operations. You should end the session with a list of general solutions, required action, dates, and responsibilities.

Examples of Solutions Generated by a Planning Session

- Install a computer to do Order Processing, Inventory Control, Accounts Receivable, and Sales Analysis. (Establish detailed requirements within 90 days, select the computer within 6 months, install it 90 days later, get everything up and running within 18 months. Responsible: Harold)
- Hold a meeting with the ABC Company to discuss lead times and service. (Meeting by September 1. Responsible: Joe)
- Interim solutions prior to getting the computer:
  - Put two people on statements to get them written sooner. (Start September 1. Responsible: Mary and Susan)
  - Publish a weekly stockout flier. (Start August 15. Responsible: Susan)
  - Redo the price list. (Complete by October 15. Responsible: Mary)

Either at the planning session or afterward, teams should be formed to lay out the specific requirements of each computer application. The requirements should include a list of functions and special reports desired, along with examples.

This process serves two purposes:

1. It vastly improves your odds of finding software that suits you because you have thought about your needs.
2. It involves your people which makes them feel important and committed to the project.

Although it takes time, a planning session will save you hours of agony and frustration later on.

DEVELOPING DETAILED APPLICATION REQUIREMENTS

Whether your goals include increasing sales, reducing inventory investment, or improving collections, you should have in mind some specific reports or functions which will help you achieve these goals. Your people can exercise considerable creativity in laying out the information they need to do their jobs better. You and they can get ideas by reading Chapter 3, by browsing through brochures of computer packages, and by seeing computer demonstrations at business shows. You can also get ideas by talking to other users and to computer salespeople. Your purpose is to define the management information you need to run your business more successfully. *Caution:* don't expect any package to have exactly what you need. Custom programming is expensive, so be prepared to give something up. A general plan, however, of the type of information which will improve your business will help you compare and evaluate package alternatives.

If one of your goals is to maintain the current billing, pricing, and discounting procedures you have established, you should have a responsible employee document these for various computer vendors. Essential procedures you use today must be accommodated by the package you select.

Be sure you prepare a thorough explanation (with examples) of any application which will involve unique or special calculations. Specifically, you should define in detail any of the following things you want your computer system to do:

Pricing
Discounting
Unit of Measure conversions (stocking, shipping, pricing, and costing)
Stock Reordering computations
Costing techniques
Back order policy and algorithmns
Accounts Receivable aging periods (if other than 30, 60, 90)
Anything else unique about your business that you would have difficulty
    explaining to a new employee

You should also gather samples of any relevant documents or reports (either currently in use or newly designed). For example, your:

Order Form
Packing Slip
Bill of Lading
Invoice
Customer Ledger
Inventory Record
Price List
Sales Journal
Aging Report
Inventory Reports
Sales Reports
Commission Reports

After you have defined the functions, calculations, reports, inquiry screens, and so on you hope will be in each application package, you should summarize everything in a comprehensive application checklist. Bear in

Figure 10-1
VOLUME CHECKLIST

Accounts Receivable	Quantity
Number of customers	————
Number of invoices/month	————
Number of cash receipts/month	————
Average invoice age (number of days unpaid)	————

Inventory Control	Quantity
Number of warehouses	————
Number of items	————
Number of product classes	————
Number of issues/month	————
Number of receipts/month	————
Number of adjustments/month	————
Number of warehouse transfers/month	————
Number of purchase orders/month	————
Average number of lines/P.O.	————
Number of single level bills of material	————

mind that no package on earth contains everything, so it is important to distinguish essential items from "nice-to-have's". Appendix B contains an application function checklist which may help trigger some ideas for you.

As you list those functions you hope to find in a computer package, it is important to be realistic. The checklist in Appendix B distinguishes functions which might be found in a simple package for a microcomputer from the more sophisticated things which can be done only on a minicomputer (or larger machine). You know what ballpark you are in, and if you have only $20,000 to spend, don't fret over the minicomputer functions.

Before you are ready to talk to computer vendors, you must also gather your business volumes for each application you want to put on the computer. The volume checklists in Figures 10-1 through 10-4 indicate which volumes you will need to determine. This will allow the computer salesman to size your hardware requirements.

Figure 10-2
VOLUME CHECKLIST

Order Processing	Quantity
Number of customer shipping addresses	_____
Number of orders/day	_____
Number of line items/order	_____
Number of days until order filled	_____
Percentage of line items back ordered	_____
Number of days on back order	_____
Number of invoices/day	_____
Number of prices for all items	_____
Number of quantity breaks for all items	_____
Number of price contracts	_____

Sales Analysis		Quantity
Sales by customers		
Year-to-date sales	yes/no	_____
Month-to-date sales	yes/no	_____
Quarter-to-date sales	yes/no	_____
12 periods sales	yes/no	_____
24 periods sales	yes/no	_____
Sales by item		
Year-to-date units sold	yes/no	_____
Month-to-date units sold	yes/no	_____

Figure 10-3
VOLUME CHECKLIST

Quarters-to-date units sold	yes/no
12 periods units sold	yes/no
24 periods units sold	yes/no
Year-to-date sales	yes/no
Month-to-date sales	yes/no
Quarter-to-date sales	yes/no
12 periods-to-date sales	yes/no
24 periods-to-date sales	yes/no
Year-to-date cost	yes/no
Month-to-date cost	yes/no
Quarter-to-date cost	yes/no
12 periods cost	yes/no
24 periods cost	yes/no
Sales by Sales Representative	
Year-to-date sales	yes/no
Month-to-date sales	yes/no
Quarters-to-date sales	yes/no
12 periods sales	yes/no
24 periods sales	yes/no
Year-to-date profit	yes/no
Month-to-date profit	yes/no
Quarters-to-date profit	yes/no
12 periods profit	yes/no
24 periods profit	yes/no

At this point, you have assembled the detailed material which defines your application needs: application function checklist, sample reports, and volumes. You can use these materials either in a formal request for proposal (RFP) or as a shopping guide when you look at various computers.

Here is a summary of the steps you should follow in defining your application requirements:

Establish goals for the company.

Hold a brainstorming or planning session to get additional requirements defined.

Work with top employees in defining information that will help them do their jobs better and achieve the company's goals.

Have one or more responsible employees document current procedures you wish to maintain.

Review available material to flesh out your ideas: Chapter 3 and Appendix B and computer application brochures for your industry.

Talk to computer users and sales reps.

See one or more computer demonstrations.

Figure 10-4
VOLUME CHECKLIST

Accounts Payable	Quantity
Number of vendors	_____
Number of invoices/month	_____
Average age of invoices	_____
Number of checks/month	_____
Number of distributions/invoice	_____

General Ledger	Quantity
Number of companies	_____
Number of general ledger accounts	_____
Number of accounting periods	_____
Number of periods history (12, 24)	_____

Payroll	Quantity
Number of employees	_____
Number of departments	_____
Number of pay periods/year	_____
Number of states	_____
Number of special deductions/employee	_____
Number of unions	_____

Prepare an application function checklist which distinguishes the essential functions you are seeking from the nonessential ones.

Gather critical volume information to be sure the computer will do the job.

Now you are ready to begin shopping in earnest. If you are on a tight budget, you may want to use this material simply as a tool in the computer store for comparing packages to see which has the most function. If you are planning to put out an RFP, it will be used by various vendors to give you a bid for modifying their packages to meet all your needs. You may want them to differentiate in their bids the costs associated with each function in case you want to reconsider how much you really want something which turns out to be costly. Appendix B provides a format which allows you to do this.

Chapter 11 will cover the preparation of an RFP.

CHAPTER

11

Preparing and Delivering a Request for a Proposal (RFP) or Buyer's Checklist

If your budget for hardware and software is large enough to attract computer sales reps to call on you, you should prepare an RFP. Many businesses hire a consultant to do this because they do not have the expertise or time to do it themselves. This can cost from $5,000 to $15,000 and still involve a lot of your time because you have to educate the consultant about your business. This chapter is a recipe for preparing your own RFP and can save you that whopping consulting fee.

If you do not want to prepare an RFP, or you are looking for a microcomputer, use this chapter to help prepare a Buyer's Questionnaire or checklist for comparing vendors. It should contain the same questions we ask the vendors to answer in their proposals, but instead of asking them in writing, you do it orally.

The RFP clearly lays out your specific application and hardware requirements and asks the computer vendors to respond with a proposal. It removes ambiguity by putting everything in writing. Later, it can be used together with the contract to define what the vendor is to supply. It is also a way of ensuring that you are comparing apples with apples when you start sizing up various vendors. They are all responding to the same information, and therefore their proposals should cover comparable functions and be easier to compare and contrast.

The RFP should supply all the information the vendors will need to prepare a proposal for hardware and software. It should request sufficient information from the vendor to allow you to evaluate alternatives and compare products, costs, and risks. Together with the proposal and contract, it will become a document of mutual understanding which reflects your position should you ever get into a nonperformance issue with the vendor.

It is important to make the document short, clear, and easy to answer and at the same time to request the information you need to make an evaluation. Computer salesmen groan when they receive an RFP because they know preparing the proposal will be time consuming and that there will be many competitors in the foray.

The more money you are willing to spend for the computer, the longer your RFP can be. If you turn out a 100-page document for a $25,000 system, you probably will not get a response. As a rule of thumb, the RFP should be no more than one page long for every $1,000 you are willing to spend. If you are looking for a personal computer or anything much under $20,000, don't bother with an RFP at all because no one will respond.

The RFP will ask the vendors to submit a price for the necessary hardware and software that meets your stated needs. If you list multitudes of application functions, the vendors will undoubtedly have to specially program many of them because no package contains everything. The more specific you are about what you want, the more likely it is that it will entail custom programming. If your budget is under $30,000 to 40,000, a great deal of custom programming may not be realistic. In that case, you can still include your long list of application requirements in the RFP, but instead of asking them to bid on doing everything, merely ask the vendors to check off those functions which are in their standard packages. This way, you avoid all custom programming and can choose the package which contains the most essential functions. If the package which comes the closest is lacking something you really want, ask for a separate bid on that item and you can see how much you really want it.

RFP (OR CHECKLIST) CONTENTS

The RFP should contain the following information:

A. Brief introduction to your business
B. Overview of your computer requirements
C. Description of application requirements (one section per application)
D. Desired implementation schedule

E. Vendor proposal contents (a list of questions the vendor should answer in his proposal)

The RFP should be accompanied by a cover letter which explains what you expect to happen during the procurement cycle. It should state when you want the proposals, whether you will meet with the vendors, and when you expect to make a decision.

The following is an outline for preparing the RFP.

A. *Brief introduction to your business:*
  1. Company name and type of business
  2. Number of years in business
  3. Key products and/or services
  4. Competitive position (competitive advantages, market share, unique aspects of your business)
  5. Seasonal characteristics of your business
  6. Organization chart (numbers of employees by job position)
  7. Key business volumes (more detailed volume information should be provided in the appropriate application section)
      a. Annual sales in dollars
      b. Annual growth rate
      c. Number of customers/clients
      d. Number of products
      e. Number of employees
      f. Number of locations
  8. Business goals, expansion plans
  9. Reasons for automating
B. *Overview of your computer requirements:*
  1. Applications to go on the computer: (Prioritize)
      a. Accounts Receivable
      b. Inventory Control
      c. Order-processing
      d. Invoicing
      e. Sales Analysis
      f. Accounts Payable
      g. General Ledger
      h. Payroll
      i. Word Processing
      j. Mailing Lists
      k. Query and Report Writer
      l. Purchase Order Management
      m. Inventory Management
      n. Financial Modeling
      o. Job Costing
      p. Other (specify)

2. Hardware requirements:
   a. Type of computer (micro, mini, supermini, and so on)
   b. Required disk storage (if you have a specific preference; if not, let them determine storage requirements from your volumes)
   c. Number of CRTs desired
   d. Type of printer
   e. Brand preferences (products recommended to you or those you have been warned to avoid)
   f. Growth capabilities (e.g. must be able to add a second CRT)
   g. Additional requirements
3. Budget
4. Vendor service requirements: (e.g., turnkey installation to include: program modifications, on-site training, and on-site hardware maintenance)
C. *Description of your application requirements:*
   Include a functional checklist, sample reports, inquiries, calculations, and critical business volumes for each application
D. *Your preferred implementation schedule:*
   1. Due date for proposals
   2. Expected computer decision date
   3. Desired computer installation date (include any restriction such as busy times of the year when you would not like the computer delivered)
   4. Application priority sequence (when you want each application up and running—no more than one per month)
E. *Vendor proposal contents* (These questions can also be used to form a Buyer's Questionnaire if you are not preparing an RFP.)
   You are requesting various computer vendors to submit a proposal recommending specific hardware and software. To assess both their products and their ability to deliver as promised, you need to request the following information from them. (Asterisks denote items not relevant if you are dealing with a computer store.)
   1. *Hardware recommendation:*
      a. Who manufactures the equipment you are recommending?
      b. How long have they been in business?
      c. What is your relationship to the manufacturer (e.g., independent sales organization, master or authorized distributor, branch sales office of the manufacturer)? How long have you maintained this relationship?
      d. What computer model are you recommending?
      e. How many of these computers have been installed in the United States?
      f. How many in this area?
      g. How many by your company?
      h. How long has it been available?
      i. What configuration of this computer model are you recommending, and what growth capabilities are there? The chart in Figure 11-1 pro-

Figure 11-1
HARDWARE CAPACITY CHART

Component	Description	Recommended Capacity	Maximum Capacity
CPU	Type of chip used (e.g., 8-bit, 16-bit, 32-bit)	64K	128K
Disk	Winchester	12 megabytes	50 megabytes
Backup	Diskette	1.2 megabytes	2.4 megabytes
Printer	Bidirectional character printer	180 CPS	Line printer may be attached
CRT	1920 character display	2 CRTs	Maximum of 4

vides a good format for the vendor to use in outlining hardware capabilities.

   j. What is the cost of the configuration you are recommending?

   k. What is the warranty period?

   l. Who provides the hardware maintenance?

  m. How much is monthly hardware maintenance?

   n. What is the computer's power requirement?

   o. How many dedicated lines are required?*

   p. Does it need special flooring or air conditioning?*

   q. How long does it take to get the computer once an order has been placed?

2. *Software recommendation:*

   a. Please review the application function requirements and indicate which functions you will be able to accommodate, whether they are part of a standard package or if they will have to be specially programmed, and the cost for any custom programming. (Include the application function checklist discussed in the last chapter. A comprehensive example is offered in Appendix B.)

   b. Who developed the application package(s) you are recommending?

   c. How long have they been available?

   d. How many users are there?

   e. What language are they written in?*

   f. What operating system will be used, who developed it, and how long has it been used?

   g. Will it support the hardware you are recommending today as well as the maximum configuration?

   h. Will the application software I buy run unchanged on a larger computer should my business outgrow this one?

   i. What is the total software cost?

j. Is this a fixed price or an estimate?*

k. What additional charges might I incur?

l. What is the software warranty period?

m. How do you resolve bugs when they occur? What are the charges? Before the warranty expires? After the warranty expires?

n. What payment terms do you offer?

o. Do you perform an acceptance test of all custom programming before expecting payment?*

p. Do you allow progress payments to ensure that the work is completed, the programs debugged, and my people fully trained before I have paid in full?

3. *Support services:*

Please describe which services you provide. Include any limits or constraints such as maximum number of training hours. If additional costs may be incurred, please estimate them. (Figure 11-2 provides a format for this information.)

4. *Additional costs:*

What additional costs do you estimate for:

a. Equipment delivery

b. Supplies

c. Other

5. *Your organization:*

a. How long have you been in business?

b. What computer products do you carry?

c. What types of businesses have you sold computers to?

d. How many customers do you have?

Figure 11-2
SUPPORT SERVICES OVERVIEW

Service	Constraints/ Maximum Time Allocated	Additional Charge (Yes/No)	Estimated Cost
Installation planning†			
Advice on supplies			
Advice on room layout†			
Conversion planning†			
Data gathering and conversion†			
Hardware installation			
Application operator training			
Hot line/emergency help for operators†			
User training†			
Documentation			

†These items are not relevant if you are dealing with a computer store.

    e. How many people do you have supporting these customers?
    1. Programmers?
    2. Trainers?
    3. Maintenance?
    4. Other?
    f. Please submit a list of references in similar businesses in this geographic area.
    g. Please submit a recent financial statement.
    h. What are your payment terms and guarantees?

The RFP in Brief

Again, the more information you request from the vendors, the fewer responses you will receive. You may want to tone this down or use the Buyers Questionnaire approach (getting the questions answered orally), particularly if you are looking for a computer under $30,000 to $40,000, and *definitely* if you are looking for a microcomputer in a computer store.

SELECTING POTENTIAL VENDORS

Once you have put together your RFP or questionnaire, you need to identify six to eight computer vendors to send it to. Some businesses will send out as many as 30 copies, but you only create headaches for yourself with this many responses. You should be able to prescreen the candidates well enough to select a limited number.

    To select potential vendors, start by calling your trade association to see if there is a recommended package for your industry. If not, call other companies in your industry, preferably in your area. Ask them what computer they use, approximately how much it costs, who supplied the software, and whether they would recommend it. If the package they have is sold and supported in your area, and the price is right, their supplier should be one of your vendors.

    Next, call other local businesses about the size of yours, and ask them what computer they use and how they like it.

    Some further questions to ask computer users include:

What computer do you have?
What is the configuration, and how much did it cost?
Who sold it to you?
What software did you buy?
Did the software do what you wanted?
Did you have changes made?

Were they made as quickly as was promised?
Were the costs what you expected?
Has the service been good?
How often has the machine gone down?
How long did it take them to get there and to fix it?
What happens when you have a software bug?
What other problems have you had?
What do you like best about the software?
What would you change?
Are you satisfied?
Would you do it again?
Would you recommend them?

If the answers are satisfactory, add these vendors to your list of candidates.

If this doesn't give you six to eight potential vendors, look in the Yellow Pages under data processing equipment and start calling. (Or go to a computer show and see the displays.)

Screening questions to ask potential computer vendors: (Asterisks denote items not relevant if you are dealing with a computer store.)

What size computers do you carry? (Ascertain if they sell the right type and size machine for you. If they are vague, ask specifically if they sell what you need: e.g., microcomputers with hard disks for under $25,000 or minicomputers with a 50 million character disk for under $50,000. Find out if their equipment is in the ballpark.)
Do you sell software as well? What applications?*
Do you do program modification and training?*
Have you ever sold a computer to a business such as mine? (Describe your business.)
Please give me the name of a customer who has a business similar to mine. (You need to be sure they really do have experience in your industry.)
How many customers do you have?
How many programmers do you have?*
How long have you been in business?

After screening ten to fifteen companies, pick the best six to eight to receive your RFP. The Vendor Screening Chart in Figure 11-3 should help you evaluate the results of your telephone canvas.

IF YOU ARE SHOPPING IN COMPUTER STORES

As was previously explained, salesmen in computer stores do not have the time or experience to extensively analyze your needs and explore alternative

Figure 11-3
VENDOR SCREENING CHART

Vendor Name and Address	Telephone No.	Talked to	Computer Size Range	Applications	(Services; Program Mods; Training)	Reference Rating	No. of Customers	No. of Programmers	No. of Years in Business

packages. A rep will probably spend 2 to 3 hours with you if he thinks you are a qualified buyer and more if he thinks you will spend over $20,000 to $30,000. He does not have the time to do a written proposal or even read an RFP.

If you are planning to shop the stores, do the following:

1. Prepare a short list of desired application functions, using Appendix B as a guide. List five to ten functions for each of your top two applications and no more than two to three functions for the other applications.
2. Prepare a questionnaire modeled after section E of the RFP outline. You will ask the salesman to answer these questions orally, not in writing.
3. Screen the potential stores by telephone to find some which have experience with your type of business and/or applications.
4. Make an appointment to go in, discuss your needs, and see a demonstration. (The best times to go are 10:00–11:00 a.m. and 2:00–4:00 p.m.)
5. Evaluate and compare alternatives as discussed in Chapter 12.

IF YOU ARE PREPARING AN RFP

No matter how clearly you write, there will be some ambiguity in your RFP. Plan on one or two meetings with each vendor to clear up details and emphasize fine points. To minimize your own time involvement, you might mail out the RFP and announce a meeting of all vendors to be held 2 weeks later. At that time, review the RFP with all of them together and entertain their questions. One or two of them may bring up things the others wouldn't have thought of. The meeting will allow you to answer the questions and ensure that all vendors have the information they need.

Each vendor will submit a written proposal in response to your RFP. You can review these using the evaluation criteria discussed in Chapter 12. Then pick the top two to four for further evaluation. Before you select the winner, you must go through the following additional steps:

1. See an operational demo of each software package they recommend.
2. Talk to three to six of their installed customers.
3. Review their financial statements, résumés, organizations, facilities, and so on to get a feel for their stability.
4. Discuss in detail their plans for modifying programs, training your people, and providing additional support.
5. Establish an implementation schedule.
6. Negotiate contract terms, support commitments, and price.

Chapter 12 deals with the evaluation process in detail.

12

Evaluating the Vendors

By now you know the importance of application software in your selection of a computer. However, since you are buying a package of software, hardware, vendor support services and people for a total price, you should consider all these things. This chapter will summarize the points to examine in each area and give you some evaluation worksheets for making comparisons. It will also give you some tips for talking to vendors, viewing demos, questioning references, and assessing overall risk.

WHAT SELECTION CRITERIA ARE IMPORTANT?

The following is a comprehensive list of issues to consider. If you are looking for a microcomputer from a computer store, the asterisks denote items not relevant.

Hardware Selection Criteria

Key issues in hardware selection are

Is it a name-brand computer?
Will it do your job?
Is the equipment reliable?
Can it be expanded to handle reasonable business growth?
Is the cost competitive?
When it breaks down (and it will), will the service be good?

Is the manufacturer stable?
Are maintenance people and spare parts locally available?
Is it user friendly?
Is it compatible to larger systems if you outgrow it?

Software Selection Criteria

When looking at software, you should consider:

Does the package contain most of the functions you require?
Is it bugfree, or is it newly on the market and untested?
Has it been used by businesses similar to yours?
Can it be modified to further suit your needs?*
Will the company that wrote the package be doing the modifications?*
Is it user friendly?
Can it be run on larger computers should you outgrow the first one?
Is there a Report Writer that can be used with it?
Will the company selling it support it in the future if changes are
    necessary?*
Is it written in a common language?

Vendor Support Criteria

Examine vendors closely to see if they have the qualifications to do the job
for you:

Will they survey your business needs and write a formal proposal?*
Do they specialize in working with the first-time user?
If they will do training, have they worked with the proposed hardware
    before?
Have they worked with the proposed software before?
Do they understand your business?
Do they have other customers like you?
Have you actually met the people who will provide the technical support
    (e.g., the programmers and trainers)?*
Does the vendor have a good reputation?
Have they been in business long enough to have a good track record (e.g.,
    several installations)?

Are they going to provide all the services the first-time user requires to get
a computer successfully up and running? For example:

Will they assist you with installation planning?*
Will they put together a schedule?*

Will they work with you in defining specific application modifications and review them with you before jumping into the programming?*

Will they do programming modifications on a fixed price basis?*

Do they provide classroom application training?

Do they provide on-site application training?

Do they warranty the software?

Do they come out immediately if you have a bug (or even better, fix the bug over a telephone connection to your computer)?*

Do they provide a hot line to help new operators with questions and problems?*

Is the documentation thorough and understandable?

Will they advise you on supplies and site preparation?

Do they provide conversion advice and assistance?*

Will they make programming changes if you want them in the future?*

People Criteria

Not be be overlooked:

Do you like the people you will be working with?

Do your future computer operators like the person who will be training them?

Cost

Cost should be the last thing you look at, but obviously the system has to be affordable!

COMPARING PROPOSALS

How do you get the answers to your questions, and how do you compare the answers in order to make a decision? The information will come from the vendors' proposals, from direct questioning, from observation, and from sleuthing, or checking references.

Chapter 11 listed those things the vendor should provide in an oral or written proposal. But essentially, you need to know:

- what hardware is being recommended
- the growth capabilities of the hardware
- the application functions that are to be supplied
- the services that will be available to you
- the specific costs of everything
- the timetables involved

And if you get a written proposal, it should reiterate your business volumes in some acknowledgment or guarantee that the recommended computer will meet your needs. (A computer store will not offer this guarantee.)

Comparing Hardware Proposed

After reading the proposals or talking to the store salesmen, use the Hardware Comparison Worksheets (Figure 12-1) to contrast hardware offerings. You will not make the final decision based on hardware, so look for acceptability. If the hardware is inadequate or the cost is too high, if there is no growth path or if anything else is unacceptable, you can eliminate the vendor. The final selection, however, should be based on software, services, and risk assessment. Remember, however, that the big ticket item is the computer

Figure 12-1
HARDWARE COMPARISON WORKSHEET

	1	2	3
Vendor Name			
Manufacturer Reputation			
Manufacturer name			
Number of years in business			
Acceptable? (yes/no)			
Equipment Reputation			
Model being recommended			
Number installed in country			
Number installed in area			
Length of time in marketplace			
Acceptable? (yes/no)			
Recommended Configuration			
CPU memory			
CRT size			
Number of CRTs			
Printer speed			
Type of disk			
Acceptable? (yes/no)			
Cost Comparison			
Cost of recommended configuration			
Acceptable? (yes/no)			
Hardware Growth			
Maximum CPU memory			
Maximum number of CRTs			
Maximum size of disk			
Larger, compatible computers?			
Acceptable? (yes/no)			

Figure 12-1
HARDWARE COMPARISON WORKSHEET (Continued)

	1	2	3
Future Configuration (What you will need in 1–2 years.)			
CPU memory			
Number of CRTs			
Printer speed			
Size of disk			
Cost			
Acceptable (yes/no)			
Environmental Requirements			
Power			
Number of dedicated lines*			
Air conditioning*			
Special floors*			
Maintenance			
Hardware warranty period			
Monthly maintenance cost			
Total maintenance cost for first 3 years			
Equipment Delivery Time			
Number of days			
Acceptable? (yes/no)			

*Not relevant for microcomputers.

itself, so don't be so swayed by the software that you buy a computer which is unreliable or one that has no growth path. You must check it out.

Comparing Software and Services Proposed

The Software and Services Comparison Worksheets (Figures 12-2 and 12-3) can be used to rank vendors on software function, services, and cost. Other issues such as package track record and growth capability are either acceptable to you or not. Since programming warranties, training, and payment terms may be negotiable, if they are unacceptable you do not need to eliminate the vendor.

ASSESSING RISK

Other factors that should be considered are more subjective. Issues such as equipment reliability, vendor competence, and software ease of use need to be assessed through questioning and observation. Questions to ask and things to look for as you go through the process of screening vendors follow. Bear in mind that you are assessing credibility. Not all the answers should be

Figure 12-2
SOFTWARE COMPARISON WORKSHEET

	1	2	3
Vendor Name			
Application Fit*			
Order Processing (1–5 points)			
Pricing and Billing (1–5 points)			
Inventory Control (1–5 points)			
Accounts Receivable (1–3 points)			
Sales Analysis (1–3 points)			
Accounts Payable (1–3 points)			
General Ledger (1–3 points)			
Financial Planning (1–3 points)			
Mailing Lists (1–3 points)			
Data Base/Report Writer (1–3 points)			
Word Processing (1–3 points)			
Total points _____			
Package Track Record			
Length of time in use			
Number of users			
Number of users on this hardware			
Acceptable? (yes/no)			
Programming Guarantees			
Software warranty period			
Acceptance test (for custom programs)†			
Progress payments (for custom programs)†			
Fixed price or estimate (for custom programs)†			
Acceptable? (yes/no)			
Growth Capability			
Will the software run unchanged on larger computers?			
Acceptable (yes/no)			
Operating System			
How long in use?			
Will run on maximum configuration?			
Will run on larger computer?			
Acceptable? (yes/no)			
Software Cost			

*List appropriate applications or even the detailed functions you are seeking. Critical applications should be worth more points.

†Not relevant for microcomputers.

silver-tongued yes words. (These questions are of particular importance if you are buying a minicomputer with custom programs. If you are buying a microcomputer, glance at the section on what to look for in a computer demonstration and review the Hardware, Software and Service Comparison Worksheets and the Evaluation Worksheet at the end of this chapter.)

Figure 12-3
SERVICES COMPARISON WORKSHEET

	1	2	3
Vendor Name			
Services Provided			
Installation planning*			
Advice on supplies			
Advice on room layout*			
Application design/programming*			
Conversion planning*			
Conversion assistance*			
Hardware installation			
Application training			
Hot line/emergency help*			
User training*			
Documentation			
Acceptable? (yes/no)			
Vendor Capabilities			
Number of years in business			
Experience in your industry			
Experience with hardware			
Number of customers			
Number of programmers*			
Number of trainers			
Number of service personnel			
Acceptable? (yes/no)			
Additional Service Costs			

*Not relevant for microcomputers.

Questions to Ask the Sales Representative

In questioning the sales representative, you are trying to assess honesty, experience, and confidence in the products and services being offered.

How long have you been in the computer field?
Have you always been in sales? Have you ever been a programmer?
What businesses similar to mine have you sold computers to?
Why are you with your current company?
What services and/or products do they provide that you think are unique?
What is your attitude toward your customers?
What is your responsibility to me after I sign an order?
Describe to me the support I will get in making the whole project successful.
What will your company do if my equipment breaks down?
What will they do to guarantee the software will work as described?

Questions to Ask the Programmer or Systems Analyst

It cannot be stressed too emphatically that it is vital to meet the person actually responsible for fitting the applications to your business. As was mentioned in Chapter 8, all too often the salesman says "Oh yeah, we can do that" (and he sincerely means it), but sadly it is not the case. In meeting the technical expert, you are trying to assess his knowledge of your business and his intelligence, experience, level of commitment, and credibility.

How long have you been in the computer field?

What businesses similar to mine have you written programs for?

What did you do for those companies (briefly)?

What is your assessment of my application needs? What will not fit in your package? (Do not get into programming details, but be sure the programmer or systems analyst has read the RFP or knows what you have been telling the salesman you need.)

Describe what you will do for my company once the order is signed.

Will you provide a schedule of tasks and a regular accounting of where you are?

Will you review sample reports, screens, and calculations with me before they are programmed to be sure they are correct?

How often will you be here before the computer arrives?

How long will it take to get my applications up and running?

In what sequence would you put the applications on the computer?

How much training will you provide my operators? (If he says, "as much as necessary," ask how much is normal and if there is a limit.)

Do you show up for appointments as scheduled?

How will I reach you if I need you?

What is your attitude toward working overtime if necessary?

Why do you work for your employer?

In your opinion, what is unique about your company?

Have you experienced any problems with the hardware recommended?

Questions to Ask the Sales Manager or Owner of the Company

Here you are assessing credibility, integrity, and commitment to customer satisfaction.

How long have you been in the computer field?

Why are you with (did you start) your present company?

What special things does your company offer the first-time user?

How long has your company been in business?

How many customers do you have?

How many other businesses like mine?

How many use the hardware you are recommending?

How many use the software?

Do you feel confident your company can provide the services and products for the cost you have put in the proposal?

Do you feel you can meet the schedule that has been arranged?

What will you do for me if the schedule slips?

What happens if you get into the project and feel you have underbid on the software?

What guarantees will you give me that everything will happen as promised?

What makes your company successful?

How long do you expect to stay in business? What are your future plans?

Why do you sell this particular hardware? How long have you sold it?

What customer complaints have you received?

Please give me the names of some happy customers and some unhappy ones. I want to see how you react to problems.

Please give me your last financial statement or last year's tax return. (He will want yours too.)

WHAT TO LOOK FOR IN A COMPUTER DEMONSTRATION

You may see a demonstration either at the vendor's office or at a user site. Each has its advantages, and it's not a bad idea to do both. But if you have to choose, a user demo is clearly preferable. You can ask candid questions about how they like the computer, and you are more likely to get a realistic assessment of its operational characteristics. Also, if you take your computer operator along, the user site will be less intimidating than the vendor's sales office.

At some point, however, you should at least visit the vendor's sales office in order to assess how substantial the business appears.

Is it in a location convenient to your office?

Is the office in a nice building or in a fleabag?

Is it clean and well-organized?

Are the people courteous and cheerful?

Do they appear to be thriving or desperate for business?

Is the company small, medium, or large in terms of the number of employees?

Does the space appear too large or too expensive for the size of the business?

If anything you see disturbs you, ask about it and see how they handle the response.

Before you go to see the demo, make a checklist of things you would like to see. In this way you can judge each vendor by your criteria. It is unrealistic to expect to see anything substantial in less than 2 hours. And unless you just want to be sold on the sizzle (not you!), plan on spending 2 or 3 hours. When viewing a demo, you should be assessing application function and ease of use, or user friendliness. Your demo checklist should include specific functions for each application as well as certain ease of use characteristics.

Application Functions

What application functions should you ask to see?

Naturally this is up to you and your interests, but you should look extensively at those operational applications which are the most difficult to fit. For example, if you are a distributor, try the following:

Enter a new customer record
Enter two or three inventory items
Enter an order
Print a picking list
Enter the quantities shipped (something different from the ordered quantity)
Print an invoice (check the pricing and format)
Display customer and inventory inquiries to see if the invoice information was posted
Enter cash receipts
Run an aging report
Enter inventory receipts
Run two or three inventory reports
Review the menus for Accounts Receivable, Inventory, and Sales Analysis, and run any reports that look unique or interesting
Look at Accounts Payable and General Ledger menus, and run anything of interest
Use the Report Writer to develop a unique report

A contractor should evaluate Job Costing. A manufacturer should look at Bills of Material, Routing, Costing, Work Order Release and Status, and so on. A law firm should evaluate Billing and Time Accounting.

As you are reviewing application function, you can also be assessing user friendliness. Let us define this and give you some things to look for.

User Friendliness

If your business is like most small businesses, you neither have nor want a professional computer staff. You want Susie or Bill to be able to operate the computer with ease and confidence, and you may even want the same for yourself. And if Susie or Bill leaves, the new person should be able to ease quickly into the operation. Most computer software today is designed with this in mind but some packages are more successful than others. Here are some important things to look for:

Computer Sign On: Weird Commands Versus English

When you see a demonstration, ask them to start by turning the computer on so you can see the entire process you will have to go through each morn- ing. The procedure of "signing on" or waking up the computer can vary all over the map. On one minicomputer it takes 15 minutes and a four page list of gibberish which has to be typed in every day. This is ridiculous. Other computers ask you in English for a password, today's date, and you're up and running.

Menus

Today most computers provide the user with menus from which you select what you want to run. The first menu (or master menu) will ask which appli- cation you wish to run. If you select Accounts Receivable, the next menu will ask if you want to post cash or run statements.

Example—Master menu:

1. ACCOUNTS RECEIVABLE
2. INVENTORY CONTROL
3. ORDER PROCESSING
4. SALES ANALYSIS
WHICH APPLICATION DO YOU SELECT?

Example—Accounts Receivable menu:

1. POST NEW INVOICES
2. ENTER CASH RECEIPTS
3. PRINT CASH RECEIPTS REGISTER
4. PRINT AGING REPORT
5. RUN STATEMENTS
WHICH JOB DO YOU WANT TO DO?

When you compare demonstrations, look at the menus to see if all the entries are clear and self-explanatory. Could you come in on a weekend alone, look at the menu, and figure out what to do? Are they well organized or clut- tered? Are the words in English or "Computerese"?

Prompting

When the computer operator is entering orders or cash receipts, does the computer prompt her with instructions? Is it clear what information she is supposed to be entering? Some systems are so straightforward that an operator can be trained in a few hours. Other systems require days and weeks to understand. Naturally, the more function you have in your package, the longer it will take to learn it, but the clarity of the computer prompts can make a huge difference in ease of use. After viewing a demo, do you feel you could enter an order with minimal assistance?

Help Messages

If you make a mistake, how does the computer respond? If you enter an invalid part number, does the system just stop or does it display a clear and understandable error message? Some computers give you a message when you goof, but it may be something like "RXX98465." You have to look this up in a book to find out it means the customer is over his credit limit. Other computers have what is called a "Help Key." If you don't understand a message you press this key, and the explanation appears on the screen. As you watch a demonstration, ask them to make some mistakes, and see how the computer responds. Can you understand the messages? Is there a Help Key if you need further explanation? Does the message include what you have to do to correct the mistake? (For example, "INVALID PART NUMBER, PLEASE PRESS THE ENTER KEY AND REKEY THE PART NUMBER".)

Backup Procedures

One of the most cumbersome, weighty, and boring things you can do (and must do) on a computer is daily backup. It can also be simple and straightforward. Ask the demonstrator to show you how it is done and to let you try it. (He will probably faint at the thought of you accidentally erasing the disk!) See how the computers you are examining vary in backup simplicity.

Documentation

With each application package you should be given books to assist with conversion planning as well as computer operation. Ideally, you would also receive programmer documentation in case you ever hire a different programmer to work with your package. At its best, documentation would include books on:

- Getting ready for the computer
- What to do to get ready for each application
- Computer operation
- Operation of each application
- Management use of computer reports
- Suggested daily and month-end schedules
- Programming details (to be filed and handed to future programmers)

Figure 12-4
DEMONSTRATION CHECKLIST

Date		Vendor	
What to Look for	Possible Points	Vendor Points	Comments
Was vendor on time for the demo?	1–2		
Was vendor well-prepared?	1–3		
Who was in attendance?			
Salesman	1		
Programmer/Analyst	1		
Owner/Manager	1		
What was your impression of vendor office?	1–3		
Was the application function adequate?*			
Entering a new customer	0–2		
Entering an item	0–2		
Entering an order	0–2		
Printing a pick list	0–2		
Entering shipped quantities	0–2		
Printing shipped quantities	0–2		
Customer inquiry	0–2		
Inventory inquiry	0–2		
Entering cash receipts	0–2		
Printing an aging report	0–2		
Printing sales reports	0–2		
Using the report writer	0–2		
Was the system user friendly?			
Sign-on procedure	1–3		
Menus	1–3		
Prompting	1–3		
Help messages	1–3		
Backup procedures	1–3		
Documentation	1–3		
Total points			

*List the functions you wish to see.

Ask to see the documentation you will be given and take a look at the nonprogrammer books. Are they comprehensible to a normal human being?

Demonstration Evaluation

Figure 12-4 can be useful in evaluating demonstrations.

WHAT TO ASK A REFERENCE?

Obviously, the purpose of talking to references is to get an objective opinion of the quality of the vendor's work and to assess credibility. You are trying to minimize your risk by taking the time to check the vendor's track record. In reality, however, most references tell a good story. First of all, people want to show off that they've done the right thing. They would have to be very unhappy to say, "I really blew it when I bought this dog." And if they were that miserable, you probably wouldn't be referred to them. However, if you ask pointed and direct questions, references will most probably answer them, and some interesting things may come to light.

Some references may be set-ups, ringers who are getting kickbacks or special service to help sell computers. To minimize the chance that you will talk only to ringers, do the following: Ask for three to six references. After you get the list, ask what industry each is in, where they are located, and how long they have had the computer. Then ask for something that is not on the list. "Don't you have any other distributors? Isn't there a customer in West Los Angeles? Can't I talk to someone who has installed the computer within the last 3 months?", and so on. When you interject new criteria, the vendor has got to come up with some unplanned names, and these will probably not be ringers.

When you call a reference, do not feel guilty about taking up his time with questions. He probably did the same thing once upon a time and if all goes well, you will be submitting to the same inquisition in the future. Introduce yourself, and ask if you can have 10 minutes of his time to help you with the second most important decision of your life. And then run through the reference checklist.

REFERENCE CHECKLIST

☐ Why did you buy the computer from X?
☐ Are you glad that you did?
☐ Which computer did you buy?
☐ What applications are you running, and are they satisfactory?
☐ Did they do program modifications?
☐ Did the programming cost more than expected?
☐ Did they meet the schedule they had agreed to?
☐ How would you evaluate their training and support?
☐ How long does it take them to return calls?
☐ How do they handle problems?
☐ Are you doing everything you bought the computer to do?
☐ How long have you had the computer?
☐ How long did it take to get everything working?
☐ Have you had to buy more hardware than was anticipated?
☐ Did you have to upgrade the computer within the first year? Within the first 6 months?
☐ How long after it was installed did it take to get the computer working?
☐ How many times has it broken down?

☐ How long does it usually take for the repair people to get out to fix it?
☐ How long does it take them to get it working?
☐ Have there been any bad surprises?
☐ Would you recommend this vendor?

Subjectively, evaluate the reference information in the following areas:

Hardware reputation/reliability (1–3 points)   _____
Application satisfaction (0–10 points)   _____
Vendor reputation/dependability (0–10 points)   _____

Based on the answers you get after calling each reference, evaluate each subjectively on hardware, applications, and vendor reliability. Then add all the reference points for each vendor, and post them on the Evaluation Worksheets (Figure 12-5). Some vendors will have more references than others, and you may choose to talk only to three or so references for each vendor. It is probably worth it to talk to as many as six for each vendor, but don't go overboard. (One businessman called 87 references before buying a computer. He kept thinking he would run across a bad one and never did!)

PUTTING IT ALL TOGETHER AND RANKING THE VENDORS

At this point, you should have read and compared proposals, talked to vendors at length, seen several demonstrations, and questioned references.

What happens if you are missing information for some of the vendors? If you are able to extract it from them with a phone call, fine. If they are not cooperative in helping you get the information you have requested, it is probably an indication of their "service conscientiousness," and you can either eliminate them or compare them to the others as they are. If a vendor is unable to show you a demonstration or give you the names of some references, that is enough to eliminate him from contention.

When you have gathered all the information you want, use the Evaluation Worksheets (Figure 12-5) to compare the results. Some people like to use a cut and dried point system for determining the winner, others just "know" whom to choose.

A simple approach of ranking all the vendors in several areas should make it easy for you to select the best one or two. A final decision should not be made until you have done some negotiating as described in the the next chapter.

Figure 12-5
EVALUATION WORKSHEET

	1	2	3
Vendor Name			
1. Hardware acceptable in all areas? (yes/no)			
2. Software acceptable in all areas?			
3. Services offered acceptable in all areas?			
4. Vendor capability acceptable?			
5. Application fit as laid in proposal?			
Total points _____			
Rank vendors			
6. Risk assessment			
People evaluation*			
Sales rep (+/−)			
Analyst (+/−)			
Owner (+/−)			
Rank vendors			
Demonstration			
Total points			
Rank vendors			
References†			
Hardware points			
Application points			
Vendor points			
Total points			
Rank vendors			
7. Costs			
Hardware costs			
Total software costs			
Estimated additional service costs			
First 3 years equipment			
Maintenance costs			
Total cost*			
Rank vendors			

*Not relevant if you are looking for a microcomputer with packaged applications from a computer store. You may want to check references if the software package is very new.

†Some vendors include additional costs for supplies, delivery and communications modems in the total. Please be sure you include the same extras for all vendors.

13

The Negotiating Process

After you have been through the evaluation process and ranked the vendors according to product, services, reputation, and cost, you are ready to begin negotiations. In the interest of time, you may choose to negotiate with only the top one or two vendors; however, those you eliminate will most assuredly come back with revised offers, and you may want to look at these as well.

Who will negotiate with you? If the vendor is a sales arm of the computer manufacturer or a large retail chain, he can negotiate almost nothing. Perhaps you can squeeze him into providing some extra services, but he will not discount the price or change his terms. He simply does not have the authority and latitude to adjust company policy.

If the vendor is an independent sales organization or an independent programming firm, he is an entrepreneur with complete freedom to wheel and deal. In fact, it is quite common for him to adjust the initial proposal one, two, or even three times in order to get the business. The smaller the vendor, the more likely he is to do this.

What is negotiable when you are buying a computer? If you are dealing with an entrepreneur, he is capable of adjusting almost anything: hardware price, software price, payment terms, guarantees, contract wording, and so on. In most cases, however, the buyer fights for the wrong concessions. Far too often the final throes of buying a computer become a squabble over price alone. There is a serious danger in this.

Why is price the least important issue? Most buyers wrongly view the *price* of hardware and software as the total *cost* in acquiring the computer. The cost of the computer can be far greater than the price tag if there are implementation problems and delays. What is the cost of the disruption of your business if the conversion does not go (fairly) smoothly? If your employees are demoralized and quit? If your customers get fed up and go elsewhere? Can you compare a few thousand dollars with the value of your reputation or the morale and commitment of your employees? Furthermore, do you want to deal with a vendor who is not making a profit? Do you think he'll be around tomorrow to support you if he is only scraping by? And do you think you'll be his top priority if you are his number one squeezer.

For these reasons, you should first concentrate your negotiations in the following areas:

- Support commitments
- Payment terms and conditions
- Contract wording

When these important issues have been worked out, you can broach the issue of a price discount. You are looking for the best possible return for the best possible price. Let's be sure you have adequately spelled out the expected return before you quibble over price.

THE SMOOTHEST POSSIBLE CONVERSION

You are a savvy executive of the eighties, and you have now read most of this book. You *know* that no one has a computer conversion that's as smooth as silk. However, the problems can definitely be minimized. While you are still in the driver's seat with your computer vendor, before you have ordered or paid him a penny, you can extract certain written commitments which will go a long way to assure your success. In addition to written commitments which will protect you legally, you can reach a level of mutual understanding with your vendor which will make him *want* to give you the support you need.

If you skipped Chapter 8 on computer disasters, you may want to read it now. The whole point of negotiations is to prevent these problems from happening to you. As was stated in that chapter, the biggest problem in the computer industry today is that there are not enough programmers or technical support people to go around. Almost every computer company is short-handed and, as much as a vendor would probably like to, he is unable to provide the best possible service to every customer. Your goal is to make yourself the vendor's top priority.

How do most computer vendors decide where to allocate their limited resources? Most vendors have A, B, and even C customers who receive support accordingly. Top priority, or A customers, are normally those who have ironclad contracts and are threatening to sue—the proverbial squeaky wheels. They may also be customers who have the potential to become excellent references or who are willing to become demo sites and help sell more computers. The optimum role to adopt is that of the "gracious squeaky wheel": reasonable, fair, appreciative of support, gracious to all the people you are working with, very willing to be a reference and demo site, but extremely firm in your expectations. And to be a squeaky wheel with clout, your expectations need to be clearly spelled out in writing.

THE WRITTEN AGREEMENT

Either the contract or an accompanying document (the RFP and/or the vendor's proposal) referred to in the contract, must specifically state what the vendor is to supply, under what conditions, over what time frame, and for what cost.

Computer stores usually sell the computer with no accompanying contract (unless you are leasing it). You get a sales slip as if you were buying a television set. However, they will often throw in such extras as training, a free program, or some supplies. They will also discount the price. If you successfully negotiate for any of these things, you will have to get a written agreement. Problems arise for both sides when things are defined ambiguously, e.g., "Vendor will install Accounts Receivable by March 1." What does install mean? That it will be on the computer? That everyone will be trained on it? That the manual system will have been completely converted to the computer? And what constitutes Accounts Receivable? Cash posting and statements? Or delinquency notices, aging reports, and inquiries?

Defining the Deliverables

You don't need to be a lawyer to know that the more clearly you define what is to be delivered, the better chance you have of receiving what you expect. In addition to hardware, you must define:

Application Function

If you are buying an application package, what you see is what you get. (Do review the package demo and documentation so you know.) The specific functions, screens, and reports for each application of custom software must be listed. If this list has been included in the RFP, the contract should refer to the RFP, stating that all functions requested will be supplied. Where you have a unique or special need, it should be defined in further detail. For example, don't merely state, "Accounts Receivable inquiry to be programmed." Instead, state, "Accounts Receivable inquiry displaying customer name and address, balance due, aged amounts due (over 30, 60, 90), and year-to-date sales will be programmed, tested, and installed by March 1."

Support

If you walk into a retail computer store and buy an application package off the shelf, you may not receive any training but you can usually negotiate for *some* if you are buying the computer as well. If you buy software from a vendor touting turnkey installations, you are buying a package of software, documentation, training, conversion assistance, debugging, and hand hold-ing. How much support you will receive is negotiable.

Most vendors like to leave the support commitment ambiguous so they can't be hung by it later and are free to shuffle resources at will. They will try to get by with words like "sufficient training" and avoid like the plague a definition of "sufficient" or a specific promise to "provide 3 days worth of on-site training." Often the buyer feels he is getting a better deal by leaving it open ended; he hopes he will actually receive as much as he needs and that this might be more than 3 days. In truth, when the support commitment is ambiguous, the buyer rarely receives as much support as he wants and needs. You and the vendor are both better off with the support clearly spelled out. If you know you are only getting 3 days of training, you will treat that time with respect and be prepared to give your trainer 100 percent. If he knows he must spend 3 days on training, he can plan his resources and orga-nize accordingly.

In addition to specifying the quantity of training you will receive, it is a good idea to list those things which will be accomplished by the training. You don't want someone to come out and gossip with your operator for the agreed upon 3 days and then say, "That's it." For example, you might put some-thing like this in the contract:

> "Regular preinstallation planning meetings should be held to thoroughly advise us on the following:
> Equipment delivery schedules
> Application design
> Programming status (in the case of custom programming)
> Computer room layout (furniture arrangement, power, air conditioning, flooring)
> Supplies to be ordered (special cabinets, forms, paper, ribbons, diskettes)
> Training and conversion plan
> Data gathering, numbering systems, file preparation
> After the computer is delivered, hands-on training should include:
> Turning the computer on and off (signing on and off)
> Loading paper, ribbon, disks and diskettes
> Performing backup and related activities
> Using the computer's utilities
> Reading the computer manuals and finding error messages
> Placing a service call
> As a result of application training, our people should be able to:
> Prepare and gather data prior to conversion
> Create master files

Enter transactions; find and correct errors
Operate all the programs within the application
Schedule which things should be done daily, weekly, and monthly and in what sequence
Balance control totals and audit trails to ensure accuracy
Read and understand the contents of all reports and inquiry screens
Use the available application manuals
In addition to on-site training on these subjects, documentation should be provided to help us get out of a jam or find an answer when the trainer is not available."

If you plan to specify in the contract the amount of support to be provided, you might be asking yourself: How much support, advice, training and hand holding will be needed? How much is realistic to expect? What should I ask for? All things being equal, support is allocated according to the amount of money you are planning to spend. If you are buying a $50,000 computer, you will clearly receive more advice and guidance than a business buying a $25,000 system. Fortunately, there is a reasonable correlation between dollars spent and support needed. A more expensive computer is more complex, and more training is necessary.

As a rough guide, you might ask for the following:

1. One preinstallation planning meeting (2 to 3 hours) for each $10,000 you are spending for hardware and software.
2. One software review meeting for each $1,000 to $2,000 you are spending on custom software.
3. One or two half-day meetings for orientation to the computer (regardless of hardware cost).
4. One application training session of 2 to 4 hours for each $500 you are spending on software. (If you are buying a microcomputer, you are more likely to get 1 or 2 hours per application. However, the documentation that comes with a micro is *better* than that which comes with a mini, so you don't need as much help.)

In short, your contract should be your insurance that you will get the support you need. The contract should specify the tasks to be performed and the amount of support to be provided, or at least include statements which define the results to be achieved through the training, such as, "Training will enable my operator to run the computer and all applications unassisted." Let your lawyer look at the contract to see if it will give you adequate protection.

IMPROVING YOUR CLOUT

If you have clearly set forth your expectations in the contract, you have a document to wave over the vendor's head if he is not performing. The most effective way to nudge him along and keep progress forthcoming, however, is to have some continuing financial clout.

There are a variety of software and hardware payment plans, ranging from cash on delivery, to progress payments for performance. Since payment terms are also negotiable, it is worth discussing some approaches.

Cash on Delivery

It is customary to pay for the hardware upon delivery. But when it comes to software, be cautious. Computer stores and major manufacturers generally sell packages which have been installed hundreds of times nationwide. But small systems houses with their own packages won't have this track record. When a locally-developed application package is delivered to your business, you may have no idea whether it is complete, free of bugs, or if you will receive sufficient training to be able to use it. It is customary to pay a deposit when a package is ordered and to make another payment when it is delivered; however, something should be retained until it is working acceptably. But if the software has been installed many times and is well proven, the vendor will usually want the money up front.

The Acceptance Test

When custom programming is involved, many vendors will do an acceptance test or an in-depth demonstration of the customer's software on the customer's hardware at the vendor's office. If everything checks out, the machine and programs are delivered, and full payment is expected. This arrangement puts maximum pressure on the vendor. He performs the bulk of the work without receiving more than a downpayment. Furthermore, if you refuse to take the computer until everything is acceptable, the vendor usually still has to pay the computer manufacturer. The financial pressure will be enormous to complete the project. Even with an acceptance test, however, there may still be bugs and problems which come to light in daily operations. It is a good idea to hold back some final software payment (10 to 15 percent) for 90 to 120 days.

Progress Payments

If the programming project lasts several months, it may be necessary to pay something as you go. You don't want the programmer to starve, but at the same time, you want to be sure there are measurable milestones being met along the way. The first month, he should design the applications he is going to develop and show you layouts of the reports and inquiry screens. Every month after, he should tell you which programs he plans to write and demonstrate their completion. You need reasonable assurance that all is progress-ing if you are shelling out the cash every month. It is wise to pace the pay-ments over the entire project (including training and documentation) and retain at least 10 to 15 percent as a final completion payment.

Penalties, Bonuses, and Completion Payments

There are many creative ways to get your vendor's attention and keep it until all your programs are successfully running. Withholding final payment until everything is checked out is one which has been mentioned. If you plan to do this, you should make it clear at the beginning to avoid negative feelings which will sour your relationship. A more positive, although more expensive approach is to offer a bonus for on-time completion and subtract something for each day's delay.

Downpayment

It is customary to make a downpayment when you order a computer. The vendor will be spending time and money on your behalf prior to the comput-er's arrival, and it is fair that he should have some money as evidence of your commitment. In some cases, this downpayment may be refundable. How-ever, if he orders a computer for you, and you cancel within 1 or 2 months of shipment, the vendor has to pay a cancellation penalty to the manufac-turer. This could well chew up your downpayment. Be sure you find out what restrictions apply if you should have to cancel.

The downpayment is normally between 20 percent and 30 percent of the hardware and software costs. If a vendor wants more than 30 percent, he may be over-committed financially, and you should be very suspicious.

Estimates, "Guesstimates," and Fixed-Price Bids

Some vendors will not give a fixed-price bid for custom programming because they have been burned by underbidding in the past. Unfortunately, this puts you in the uncomfortable position of buying a computer without knowing the total cost. If a vendor will not give a guaranteed fixed bid, occa-sionally he will offer a "not to exceed" upper limit. One company gives an estimate and charges only one-half the normal hourly rate if they exceed it. But no matter what a vendor offers to assuage you, you are still safest with a fixed-price bid.

Many programming estimates are made by the seat of the pants so either the customer or the vendor may end up dissatisfied. It is very difficult to give a cursory look at someone's business and estimate either package modifi-cations or custom programming with any accuracy. And if the vendor guesses low, even if he offers you a fixed bid, you can end up with problems. If he gets into the middle of a sticky project and finds that he cannot possibly complete it and make money, he may walk away. You can always sue, but it can take years (and pots of money) to resolve a problem through the courts. So it is to your mutual benefit that he make a very thorough study before presenting a bid and that the price be fair to all sides.

If you have prepared an RFP, you have a good starting point for spelling out your needs. But the RFP has only listed business functions to be auto-mated, not fleshed them out in detail. It is comparable to a description of a home (e.g., two bedrooms, two baths, living room and kitchen) and not to a blueprint used for construction. To estimate programming hours accurately, application functions, reports, screens, and computations must be fleshed out, or designed. That is, in fact, the first step of any programming project. If you are not in a time bind to get the computer, it is an excellent idea to pay the number one vendor to design the custom programming in detail before you order the computer. Once he has done the design, he can give you a very accurate bid for the programming. If you don't like his bid, since you now own the design you can ask other vendors to bid on the work.

In most cases, the vendors will make a bid without doing this detailed design in advance, and the customer will go ahead and order the computer, trusting that the work can be completed in the time promised. While you are waiting for the computer, you should insist that the design be completed and reviewed with you before any programming begins. It is the best way to force the vendor to begin the project and to be sure that he really understands what you want.

Invariably you will see something you want changed. It is as crucial as looking at blueprints before you begin building a house. After the house is finished, it is too late to move the bathroom out of the kitchen.

Project Completion

While you are thinking about methods of paying for your programming, it is worth considering what constitutes project completion. You obviously do not want to finish paying for something that isn't complete. Many people limp along forever with programs that still have a few bugs or aren't quite right. This can be minimized if you will spend the time to do the design reviews just mentioned. No two people can communicate perfectly, and your pro-grammer is bound to have misunderstood something you have asked for. If you are in frequent communication and review his work at regular intervals, you will catch things in time to correct them.

After he designs the programs, the programmer will write and test them. The testing process is crucial. You want to make the test examples as realistic as possible and include all the exceptions, problems, and errors which could challenge and "blow" your programs. It is the programmer's responsibility to do the testing, but he will ask you and your people for help to be sure all conditions have been tested. For example, in the complex area of your pricing and discounting, what exceptions and strange situations can and do come up?

After the programs have been thoroughly tested, your people will have to be trained to run them, and your business procedures will have to be converted to the new system. You will also need written instructions, or documentation. Before you can be sure that everything is satisfactory, you must run these programs for at least a month, and preferably for 90 days. It can take that long to run across obscure situations the programs do not handle properly.

The contract should specify what constitutes project completion: programming, testing, training, converting, documenting, and successful operation for a reasonable period of time (30 to 90 days). Full payment should not be made until the project is completed. If the vendor's terms cannot be negotiated and you must pay in full before you have used the programs during a trial period, at least be sure that the software is warrantied.

Warranties

The software warranty should ensure that the vendor will fix any obvious bugs at no charge to you for a specified period of time. The time may vary from 30 days to 1 year, but 90 days or more is highly desirable. Warranties apply to package as well as to custom software. A warranty does not mean that the vendor will improve or change the software to suit your every request, only that he will fix hard errors. If a package has been out and tested for a lengthy period, there may no longer be a warranty. This should not concern you if the package has a good track record.

In the case of custom software, there can be a gray area between bugs and requests. You may find the software unsatisfactory because you assumed it should include certain information on a specific report. The vendor may never have understood that you wanted this feature. This kind of misunderstanding can be minimized with the design review procedure described earlier. A professional programming firm will get you to sign off on custom programs after using them for 30 to 90 days. After this acceptance, any additional changes you request are billable.

Hardware warranties are normally determined by the manufacturer and passed on to you. The most common warranty is 90 days for parts and labor. This is usually not negotiable.

Maintenance

After the hardware warranty expires, an ongoing maintenance contract is a good idea. Computers (particularly minis and larger) contain some expensive parts, and you don't want to have to pay to replace one of them. Furthermore, when your computer becomes an integral part of your operation and then breaks down, you want it fixed ASAP. If you have a maintenance contract, you will receive priority attention.

Monthly hardware maintenance for minicomputers normally costs about 1 percent of the hardware price; for micros, it runs about 1.5 to 2 percent. You usually sign up for 1 year at a time, and pay in advance.

Some companies offer maintenance contracts on application software after the warranty expires. They normally charge 10 percent of the software cost per year. Services might include new updates of the software, hot line support to help you with operator problems, training for new operators, and discounts on programming expenses or future applications. Computer stores do not now offer this type of long-term involvement with their customers.

Small independent computer companies are wise to offer software maintenance. It enables them to develop a long-term relationship with their clients. They have a steady revenue stream from the maintenance contracts, which allows them to increase staff to provide ongoing support. If your computer vendor offers a software maintenance contract, it is a plus.

Extra Charges

Things do not always go according to plan. You may need extra programming or training which is not spelled out in the contract. You may want a program fixed or changed after the warranty period has expired. You should be sure you know the rates for these services before signing the contract.

Fixing Bugs

Whether you are under warranty or you are paying for his help, you will have programming bugs, and you will want the vendor to fix them ASAP. Some of the more professional programming firms insist that you buy a communications "modem" for your computer. This device allows the programmer to call your computer from his office and make programming changes without having to come in person. The advantages are enormous: you get prompt service, and he saves time. Encourage your vendor to adopt this approach.

Contract Summary

Specifying payment terms, support commitments, and warranties can be as important as defining the product and services to be delivered.

In short, the contract should clearly cover everything the vendor is to provide, costs, and timetables:

Hardware
Application functions and completion schedules
Specific support services, provisions, limitations, and dates
Comprehensive costs
Payment terms
Warranties
Maintenance
Definition of responsibilities

THE BUSINESS RELATIONSHIP

While the contract is important, so is the business relationship you establish with your vendor. If you have negotiated a tough and explicit contract, he will respect you as a tough, fair, and demanding customer. However, the daily decisions he makes about the allocation of limited resources are made subjectively, and other factors enter into the equation.

Every computer sales organization is interested in establishing excellent references. A top reference is not only a satisfied user, but one who is willing to talk to new prospects and give demonstrations, and who is able to tell a credible and persuasive story. If your computer vendor believes you will be both willing and able to help him in the future, you will clearly command his attention. If you also have a tough contract, you are effectively wielding both the carrot and the stick.

Besides agreeing to be a reference, you might write a testimonial letter. Show it to the vendor and tell him he can have it when you are completely satisfied. Introduce him to your CPA and tell him that if he does the right job for you, your CPA will bring him more potential customers. This is not a suggestion that you accept kickbacks from sales or do anything unethical. But if your vendor knocks himself out to make you successful, it is reasonable to help him. If you let him know in the beginning that you will help him later, it does give him an extra incentive.

As you begin to work with your programmer, establish a good relationship with him as well. Programmers often feel unappreciated, and to a certain extent, used. The sales representative commits him to perform in a way which may or may not be realistic, and the customer expects perfection. Programmers are rarely praised and usually take all the heat for the things that invariably go wrong. They are often more comfortable with programs than with people and so do not go out of their way to establish rapport with their customers. If you can establish that rapport by showing appreciation and interest in your programmer, you will have a loyal supporter who will go far beyond the call of duty for you. To a certain extent, they control their own schedules, and if you become a favorite customer, you will get some extra help.

Effective care and feeding of your programmer include the following: make sure you and your people respect the programmer's time and put aside other activities while he is there; be prepared for his visit and do not allow constant interruptions; make an effort to keep all appointments and at the first meeting ask him to make a similar effort. If you must cancel or delay an appointment, give him as much notice as possible and ask him to do the same. As was mentioned earlier, ask the programmer to review with you all inquiries and reports before he begins actual programming. Also review his programming schedule periodically. Show interest in the progress. Each time you see him ask what has been accomplished, when you will see him again, and what he will be doing in the interim. Let the programmer know you are closely following progress and expect a great deal, but you appreciate everything he is doing for you. Do not take him for granted. Offer to write a letter of commendation if he is doing exceptional work for you. Programmers perform best for people who manage projects most closely and who expect excellence, but show their appreciation.

BUYING A COMPUTER WHEN THE ECONOMY IS ROUGH

If your business is clearly on the raw edge of disaster, you may not view it as an opportune time for a computer. When times are tough, most businesses tighten their belts and do not contemplate any new and unusual expenses. But if times are tough, and your business isn't suffering too badly, this might be the best time to get a computer. First of all, it is a buyer's market so you are in the best possible negotiating position. The vendors you are talking to all want your business—badly. And they have the time to support you well. Secondly, when your business volumes are off a bit, it is easier to make the conversion to a computer. Your people aren't as busy. Finally, if you believe in the benefits of automation, you may actually run your business more effectively with a computer. It may help you weather the storm.

SAVING A FEW BUCKS

When you have negotiated all of the commitments, terms, and conditions you want to see in the contract and you are comfortable that the deal is sound, you may want to ask for a price reduction. If you are dealing with an independent sales organization, they may be willing to drop the total price by 5 percent or 10 percent. Their hardware margins are 30 to 45 percent, depending on the volume they are doing. On the software and services, they are probably making 50 percent to 75 percent. Of course, their overhead and the sales rep's commission are coming out of this, so you don't want to squeeze too much. If they are more expensive than their competitors, you should ask for a price reduction, but if they are clearly superior to the others, their price may be justified.

One businessman asked for a discount and effectively gave it back to the vendor. He asked for a $3,000 price reduction, but then said he would return it as a bonus if the installation went smoothly and was on time. He said he would remove $100 of the bonus for every day of delay. Half the bonus went to the vendor and half to the programmer. Needless to say, everyone did his utmost for this businessman.

If you feel that the price is too high, and you want to ask for a discount, consider the following. The hardware margin is a function of the manufacturer's policy and the vendor's sales volume. If the vendor has represented the manufacturer for several years, and they sell over 25 computers a year, there is a good chance they receive one of the higher margins (40 to 45 percent and even 50 percent). In this case, a discount of 5 percent on the hardware may be reasonable. (Computer stores may offer 10 percent off.) The independent vendor is free to do this if he chooses.

The second area to look at is the software price. Vendors will probably not discount programming fees for custom software because this is an area where they may be nervous about making a profit at all. However, if you are buying standard packages which they own, they may have already spread the cost of developing those packages over previous customers. If the packages have been in use for over 1 year, and particularly if they have been around for 2 or 3 years, you can ask for a price reduction. But be sure they are making more than enough to cover their training and hand-holding costs, or you will get shortchanged in that department. Computer stores generally have a 50 percent margin on software, so again they might allow you 10 percent off. The best time to ask for software discounts is when you buy the computer. Later on, they have little incentive to wheel and deal.

Normally, the only person who can agree to a price reduction or any change in policy is the manager or owner of the company. When you get to the advanced stages of negotiations, be sure you get the top person involved. And please remember that negotiating software and service commitments, effective payment terms, and length of warranties is far more important than shaving a few dollars off the price—particularly if you expect extensive programming or training from the vendor.

14

Financial Considerations

You have selected the best computer and are almost ready to order. You want to be sure you know how much it's *really* going to cost and how to pay for it before you sign on the dotted line. The purchase price of the computer and software programs is not your only expense, and you clearly want as few financial surprises as possible. Consider the following expenses, and if your computer vendor did not include them in the proposal, ask him to help you determine how much they will be.

"NO HIDDEN EXPENSES" CHECKLIST

☐ Total cost of hardware configuration
☐ Total cost for software (including operating system, languages, utilities, application packages, and required modifications)
☐ Upgrade cost to expand the computer to meet future business growth requirements
☐ Cost of follow-on application packages
☐ Additional cost (if any) to fully train at least two of your operators (usually included)
☐ Additional cost to train your management and accounting staff on the use of the computer system and the purpose of all reports provided (usually included)
☐ Additional cost for documentation or extra copies of the manuals (one or two copies usually included)
☐ Fees for future custom programming or package modification (usually $25 to $50 per hour)

☐ Fees for future operator training (usually $25 to $35 per hour)
☐ Hardware maintenance charge (usually 1 to 1.5 percent of hardware cost per month, often payable in advance annually after hardware warranty expires)
☐ Software maintenance charge (usually 10 percent of the software price per year, payable in advance after software warranty expires)
☐ State Sales Tax (applies to both hardware and software)
☐ Freight (normally 1 to 2 percent of hardware cost)
☐ Start-up supplies such as diskettes, disks, printer ribbons, computer paper, and so on (anywhere from $300 to $1,000)
☐ New furniture such as tables for the CRTs and special file cabinets
☐ Special new continuous forms such as invoices, statements, checks, and so forth (depending on quantity, multiple parts, artwork, and so on costs can range from $0.02 to $0.20 per form; invoices tend to be about $0.04 to $0.08 each)
☐ Site preparation (expense for special air conditioning, bringing in new power lines, building construction, and so on; difficult to estimate here)
☐ Insurance for hardware, software, and the protection of your computerized business records from fraud or accidental erasure (a new business offering)
☐ Expense for bringing in extra temporary help to assist with the conversion (normally $10 to $15 per hour; your vendor should be able to estimate the amount of help you will need and recommend either specific individuals or an agency)
☐ Overtime expense for your own people during the conversion
☐ Travel expense for you to leave town during the conversion!

HOW DO YOU PAY FOR IT ALL?

The first decision to be made by most small businesses is whether to lease, rent, or buy the computer and its programs. After this decision has been made, the question of which additional expenses can be bundled into the lease or purchase package remains.

Normally services such as programming and training are payable as they are incurred and are expensed as such. However, if you are dealing with a single source vendor, he may bundle hardware, software, modifications, training, and even a supply starter kit into one package. This package can then be financed or leased. You are also eligible for the Investment Tax Credit on both hardware and software if you buy them from the same source, and they are invoiced as a package. (Otherwise, some CPAs advise that you can take a tax credit only on hardware because software has not been approved by the IRS as tangible personal property.)

Considerations in Leasing

If you buy your computer directly from the manufacturer, he may offer a lease plan. Otherwise, you will probably arrange your lease through a third party. Computer leases are normally for 60 months with a small buy out at the end of the term (anything from $1.00 to 10 percent of the computer's initial cost). Originally, computer lease plans provided you with a great deal of flexibility and protection from computer obsolescence. At any time during the lease you were able to change to a different computer with no penalty. Under most small computer lease plans today, you are obligated for the entire term of the lease. It is essentially a conditional sales contract, an alternative to going through your bank to purchase the computer. However, in one sense it is less flexible than normal banking terms: There is a hefty, prepayment penalty for paying off the lease in the early years because you will still have to pay a good chunk of the total interest.

Leasing requires no downpayment, so if cash is tight, this may be preferable to purchasing. Nevertheless leasing may be more expensive than purchasing. You will be quoted a monthly leasing fee rather than an interest rate, but the effective interest rate is often higher than that offered by your bank. When you lease a computer, you can usually choose whether or not to take the investment tax credit. The lease rate will be lower if you do not take the ITC.

Considerations in Purchasing

A purchased system offers greater tax benefits in the early years with the accelerated cost recovery system. In actual after tax dollars, purchasing will cost less than leasing, but it requires more money up front. If you purchase with bank financing, the terms are normally 10 percent to 20 percent down, 60-month financing, and 2 points over Prime.

Considerations in Renting

Very few computer vendors allow you to rent a computer. Renting is clearly the most expensive way to acquire a computer but it provides you with the most flexibility because you can usually get rid of the computer with 30 to 90 days notice. Naturally, this gives you maximum leverage with your vendor.

What Can You Expect to Pay after Taxes?

The examples in Figures 14-1 and 14-2 illustrate the after tax cost of purchase. They are offered to give you an idea of the analysis which can be done and are not meant to be an exact projection of your expenses. Ask your computer salesman to complete this kind of spreadsheet for you. He can also draw up a comparison between leasing and purchasing, using current rates. Review these with your CPA before deciding which route to take.

Figure 14-1
COMPUTER PURCHASE COST FACTORS*

Amount of investment:	$30,000
Downpayment required by bank:	10%
Bank's interest rate:	18%
Number of months to be financed	60
State income tax rate	10%
Federal income tax rate	40%
Length of hardware warranty	90 days
Length of software warranty	1 year
Hardware maintenance	$205/month
Software maintenance	$800/year

For a Leasing Analysis, you would also need to know:
Number of months of lease
Monthly rate
ITC available to you? (yes/no)
Buy-out cost at end of lease

Figure 14-2
COMPUTER PURCHASE COST ANALYSIS, IN DOLLARS

	Year 1	Year 2	Year 3	Year 4	Year 5	Total
Cash Out						
Downpayment*	3,000					3,000
Bank payments						
Principal	3,660	4,375	5,232	6,254	7,479	27,000
Interest	4,568	3,852	2,996	1,972	749	14,137
Hardware maintenance	1,845	2,460	2,460	2,460	2,460	11,685
Software maintenance	0	800	800	800	800	3,200
Additional expenses	615	0	0	0	0	615
Total Cash Out	13,688	11,487	11,488	11,486	11,488	59,637
Deductible Expenses						
Interest	4,568	3,852	2,996	1,972	749	14,137
Depreciation (ACRS)†	4,500	6,600	6,300	6,300	6,300	30,000
Hardware maintenance	1,845	2,460	2,460	2,460	2,460	11,685
Software maintenance	0	800	800	800	800	3,200
(State Tax Savings)‡	0	(1,153)	(1,256)	(1,130)	(1,040)	(4,579)
Additional expenses	615	0	0	0	0	615
Total Deductible Expenses	11,528	12,559	11,300	10,402	9,269	55,058
Recoverable Cash						
Investment Tax Credit	3,000					3,000
Federal Tax Savings	4,611	5,024	4,520	4,160	3,708	22,023
State Tax Savings	1,153	1,256	1,130	1,040	927	5,506
Total Recoverable Cash	8,764	6,280	5,650	5,200	4,635	30,529
Summary						
Total Cash Out	13,688	11,487	11,488	11,486	11,488	59,637
Total Recoverable Cash	8,764	6,280	5,650	5,200	4,635	30,529
True Cost/Year	4,924	5,207	5,838	6,280	6,853	29,108
True Cost/Month	410	434	486	523	571	

*Substitute total purchase price if you are paying cash for the computer.

†Under the new tax law, a computer is depreciated over 5 years at the following percentages per year: Year 1: 15 percent, Year 2: 22 percent, Years 3 to 5: 21 percent each year.

‡State Tax savings are taxable by the IRS, so are shown as a negative deduction in the following year. The negative deductions may actually take place in the same year, but they are shown this way for simplicity.

What to Do After Ordering a Computer

15

Planning for the New Arrival

You may feel that the most difficult aspect of buying a computer is taking out your pen and signing the order. While that may take the most courage, it really is the easiest thing you'll have to do. If you've done the job properly, you've spent considerable time before that point going through the evalua-tion and negotiation process. But before you breathe a sigh of relief and say, "Thank goodness, that's all over," be aware that there is more to come. For the next few months, it is critical that you stay involved.

A considerable number of studies have been made on what makes one computer installation more successful than another. Invariably, they agree that the most crucial ingredient to success is the continuing involvement of management in the planning and implementation process. If you have a writ-ten plan and insist on regular weekly or biweekly progress reviews with your people and your vendor (if he is still involved with training or programming), you will keep them moving forward on the project. You will also be sure that the myriad tasks for which you are responsible do not slip through the cracks.

The planning sheets (Figures 15-1 to 15-13) will help you when working with your vendor prior to the computer installation. They cover all the things which have to happen before your computer is successfully up and running. Even the most experienced computer companies will overlook some of these, but if you hold regular meetings and review these worksheets, nothing should be forgotten.

Figure 15-1
SUGGESTED REVIEW MEETING SCHEDULE

Meeting Number	Topics for Review/Action	Schedule Date	Actual Date
1	Review installation schedule Review application sequence Identify/Commit required space		
2	Review/approve application design, programming schedule Review data gathering forms (should be supplied by vendor) Establish numbering systems; coding schemes		
3	Review/approve computer room plan Order forms, supplies, disk packs, storage equipment Review data gathering progress		
4	Approve/finalize application design Review programming schedule Set up test schedule		
5	Review conversion plan		
6	Review application progress Finalize conversion plans and procedures Review progress on machine room preparations		
7	Post installation review		

If you buy a micro from a computer store, you will probably have instant delivery of the computer and the programs. You will not have custom programs or much to worry about with site preparation. However, you will need to plan for conversion. The starred items are not relevant to you in this case.

WHAT ARE THE WORKSHEETS AND HOW TO USE THEM?

A. Suggested Review Meeting Schedule (Figure 15-1)*
Beginning 2 or 3 months before the computer is to be delivered, regular review meetings with your vendor should start. This schedule will give you an idea of which topics should be reviewed and when.
B. Installation Schedule (Figure 15-2)
The major to dos, such as ordering supplies and preparing the machine

Figure 15-2
INSTALLATION SCHEDULE

Responsible	Task	Months Before				-0-	Months After			
		4	3	2	1	-0-	1	2	3	4
	Machine delivery date determined	X								
	Application sequence determined	X								
	Project leader identified	X								
	Application design reviewed		X							
	Program development begun		X							
	Physical planning completed		X							
	Conversion planning completed			X						
	Forms, supplies ordered			X						
	Conversion completed									
	Application 1						X			
	Application 2							X		
	Application 3								X	
	Application 4									X
	Application 5									
	Application 6									

room,* must be scheduled so they are not forgotten. It is the vendor's responsibility to complete this schedule.

C. Application and Development Plan (Figure 15-3)*
If the vendor is doing any custom programming for you, ask him to complete this detailed schedule so you can review his progress at each review meeting.

D. Computer Room Plan (Figures 15-4 through 15-8)
Once you have decided where to put the computer, you will have to decide how to arrange the room. You must have your electrician bring in

Figure 15-3
APPLICATION AND DEVELOPMENT PLAN
Project Schedule

Application Name/s: _____

Task	Est. Days		Week No.	1	2	3	4	5	6	7	8	9	10	11	12	13	14	15	16
			Week Ending																
Document current procedures		Plan																	
		Actual																	
Determine objectives and develop detail plan		Plan																	
		Actual																	
Develop general system design		Plan																	
		Actual																	
Develop detail system design		Plan																	
		Actual																	
Design screen and report formats		Plan																	
		Actual																	
Review design		Plan																	
		Actual																	
Code, compile, test, document programs		Plan																	
		Actual																	

150

Develop run book	Plan																				
	Actual																				
Develop conversion plan	Plan																				
	Actual																				
Conduct training	Plan																				
	Actual																				
Convert files	Plan																				
	Actual																				
Conduct pilot run	Plan																				
	Actual																				
Conduct parallel operation	Plan																				
	Actual																				
	Plan																				
	Actual																				
	Plan																				
	Actual																				
	Plan																				
	Actual																				
	Plan																				
	Actual																				

the proper power lines and install the correct connectors,* and you may need special air conditioning or flooring.* To assist you with this planning, there are several specific forms (Figures 15-4 to 15-8).

Form	Responsible for Completion	Purpose of Form
Site preparation* (Fig. 15-4)	You	To be certain site is prepared on time
Space planning (Fig. 15-5)	Vendor	To be certain everything fits in room
Room layout (Fig. 15-6)	You	To be certain everything fits in room
Environmental plan* (Fig. 15-7)	Vendor	Give to air conditioning contractor
Electrical planning* (Fig. 15-8)	Vendor	Give to electrician

*Not relevant if you buy a micro from a computer store.

Figure 15-4
COMPUTER ROOM PLAN
Site Preparation

Task	Date
☐ Room layout form completed	_/_/_
☐ Machine room identified; size _____sq. ft.	_/_/_
☐ Additional space identified (storage, work space)	_/_/_
☐ Electrical planning form completed by vendor	_/_/_
☐ Environmental planning form completed by vendor	_/_/_
☐ Physical planning review with vendor	_/_/_
Machine room layout	
Air conditioning	
Power requirements	
Machine delivery requirements	
Elevator adequate	
Doorway large enough	
Meet with contractors	
☐ Electrical	_/_/_
☐ Air conditioning	_/_/_
☐ Electrical work scheduled	_/_/_
☐ Electrical work completed	_/_/_
☐ Air conditioning work scheduled	_/_/_
☐ Air conditioning work completed	_/_/_

Figure 15-5
COMPUTER ROOM PLAN
Space Planning

Description	Width*	Depth*	Sq. Ft.	X	No. Units	=	Total Sq. Ft.
Line printer	___	___	___	X	___	=	___
Serial printer	___	___	___	X	___	=	___
CPU	___	___	___	X	___	=	___
Disk cabinet	___	___	___	X	___	=	___
Work stations	___	___	___	X	___	=	___
Magnetic tape unit	___	___	___	X	___	=	___
Desks and chairs	___	___	___	X	___	=	___
File cabinets	___	___	___	X	___	=	___
Other	___	___	___	X	___	=	___
_____	___	___	___	X	___	=	___
_____	___	___	___	X	___	=	___
_____	___	___	___	X	___	=	___
_____	___	___	___	X	___	=	___
_____	___	___	___	X	___	=	___

Total floor space for equipment (Room should be 60% to 80% larger) ___

*Service clearance space included.

Figure 15-6
COMPUTER ROOM PLAN
Room Layout

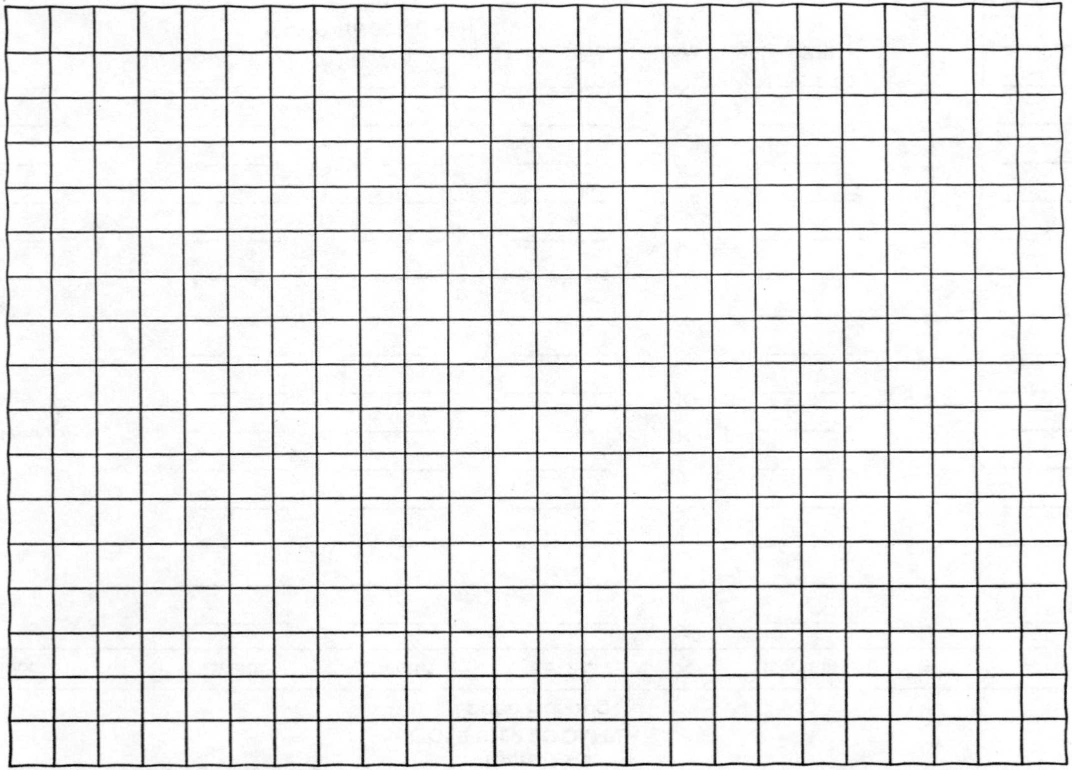

Scale: 1 square = 1 sq.ft.
Room: 17 ft. x 24 ft.

Diagram should include the following:
Location of specific machines

Figure 15-7
COMPUTER ROOM PLAN
Environmental Plan

Description	Quantity	BTU/Hr	Total BTU	Total Wt.	Recommended Temp. F°	Recommended Humidity %
Central processing unit						
Disk cabinet						
Work station						
Line printer						
Serial printer						
Magnetic tape unit						

Figure 15-8
COMPUTER ROOM PLAN
Electrical Planning

Model	Description	Required Amps	Voltage	Phase	Freq.	Connector Type	Dedicated Line Reqd?
	Central processing unit						
	Disk cabinet						
	Work station						
	Line printer						
	Serial printer						
	Magnetic tape unit						

E. Conversion Plan

To become operational on the computer, your business must go through what is called a conversion. First, information about your customers, inventory items, vendors, and so on must be gathered and then keyed into the computer. Your vendor should give you guidance with this. You must establish customer, inventory, or vendor numbers and special classification codes to use for pricing or sales analyses. Then, each application (or accounting procedure) must be put on the computer. You should not plan to put more than one application per month on the computer, because it takes time for your people to learn the new procedure. Often, they will do a "parallel" conversion—continue the old procedures at the same time they are inaugurating the new. This gives you an opportunity to carefully check out the results, but puts a real burden on your people. To assist you in scheduling these activities, there are two forms:

1. File Conversion Checklist (Fig. 15-9)

2. Application Conversion (Fig. 15-10)

These should be completed by your vendor after he consults with you.

F. Things to Order

Before you can use the computer, you need some necessary supplies: paper, printer ribbons, disks or diskettes, special continuous forms such as invoices; and perhaps some additional furniture. These things can have a lead time of 2 to 8 weeks, so order them early. To assist you in your planning, you can use these forms:

1. Supply Planning (Fig. 15-11)

2. Special Forms Plan (Fig. 15-12)

3. Storage Equipment/Furniture (Fig. 15-13)

These checklists presented in Figures 15-1 through 15-13 should help you stay on top of everything and ease the overall transition to automation.

Figure 15-9
CONVERSION PLANNING

File Conversion Checklist

File Name _____
Estimated Number of Records _____

Activity	Estimated Time	Planned Start	Planned Complete	Actual Start	Actual Complete	Person Responsible
Design file format						Programmer
Design data gathering forms						Programmer
Gather data						You
Key data						You

Figure 15-10
CONVERSION PLANNING

Application Conversion

Application Name _____

Responsible	Task	Planned Completion Date
	Complete program development, quality control and documentation	
	Establish numbering system (i.e., customer number, part number)	
	Complete operator training for building master files	
	Build master files	
	Complete operator training for daily/weekly/month-end operations	
	Establish controls for pilot/parallel run	
	Establish daily/weekly schedule	
	Complete pilot/parallel run	
	Convert	
	Reinforce operator training for month-end	

Figure 15-11
THINGS TO ORDER
Supply Planning

Suggested Initial Quantity	Item Description	Unit of Meas.	Price/ Unit of Meas.	Qty. Ord.	Ext. Price	Date Ordered	Scheduled Delivery Date
	Paper—Continuous Forms 14⅞ in. x 11 in. Parts wt. sheets						
1 18 3,000							
2 15 1,500 carbon							
2 15 1,700 carbonless							
3 15 1,000 carbon							
3 15 1,100 carbonless							
4 12 750 carbon							
4 12 800 carbonless							
	Mag tape						
	Ribbon						
	Disk packs						
	Diskettes						

Figure 15-12
THINGS TO ORDER
Special Forms Plan

Application	Form	Date Required	Designed	Approved	Order Received

Figure 15-13
THINGS TO ORDER
Storage Equipment/Furniture

Item	Quantity	Vendor	Order Date	Expected Delivery Date
CRT table				
Disk pack cabinets				
Diskette cabinets				
Tape cabinets				
Printout cabinets				
Printout holders				
Extra shelves				

16

Executive Considerations

Clearly, your involvement in the entire process of selecting and implementing a computer system is critical to the success of the whole project. Too often in small businesses, the tail wags the dog. The computer programmer tells the owner of the company what can and cannot be done on the computer, and when. If the computer is going to meet your needs, you must be involved in the selection process. You may delegate lots of the legwork to your accounting staff, but if you take some interest early on, you will achieve far greater results. First, you will get in your two cents on what the computer should do. Second, your people will know that it is important and that you are 100 percent behind the whole project. This will go a long way toward increasing their enthusiasm.

WHEN AND HOW SHOULD YOU GET INVOLVED?

Setting Objectives

Only management can and should set the broad objectives for the business and thus, for the computer. You know whether your priorities for the business include increasing sales, or improving asset management, or both. You should have concrete, measurable goals established and an idea of the information you need to help you achieve these goals. Chapters 3 and 10 will help you in this process.

Selecting the Computer

You may choose to delegate the fact-finding activities to your controller or to a selection team. These would include laying out your software requirements, writing an RFP, reading the proposals, and evaluating the vendors. But you should review the RFP before it goes out and ask your staff to explain their evaluation of the vendors after they have received the proposals. And you should definitely be involved in the negotiations.

Implementing the Computer

After the computer is ordered, you may appoint a project leader to stay on top of the conversion and run the periodic review meetings. He should keep you informed of progress on a weekly basis. If there are any problems, you will probably have to get into the act. You should both review the application design for any custom programming.

Getting Your People Excited

Computers are made or broken by the people who use them. They are, after all, nothing but a tool for people. If your employees are against the whole thing, it absolutely will not work. Period. Therefore it is worth spending some time encouraging their enthusiasm.

Your employees' first fear will be that the computer will replace them. This will be followed by their complete conviction that they will never master the beast; even if the computer doesn't take away their jobs, it will somehow get them fired anyway. The best way to combat these feelings is to have a company meeting as you start to look for a computer. Explain why you have decided to get a computer, what your business objectives are, and when you expect to put it in. Tell your employees you want them all to stay on and that you are looking for the kind of computer that is specifically for first-time users, not data processing pros.

During the selection process, let your future operators see some of the demonstrations. Ask them which machine they like. Let them meet the people who would be training them and see if they establish some rapport. Ask your key managers and accounting people to help determine the computer application requirements and to get involved in the software evaluation.

When you select a computer, ask the vendor to teach a 1 or 2 hour computer concepts class for all your employees and to share with them a little bit about the computer you have chosen. Launch a name the computer contest and give a prize for the best name.

The point is, let your people know that you want and need a computer, but that you still care about them.

When Things Go Wrong

You or your appointee should be having regular review meetings with the vendor to be sure everything is proceeding properly. If things fall behind schedule, get vendor management involved. As mentioned in the chapter on negotiating, you can keep progress flowing by withholding payment, by offering a special bonus, by offering to be a reference and demo site once everything is complete, and by threatening to sue (last resort). These things should be established when you order the computer, but do not hesitate to bring them up frequently if you are not getting results. Squeaky wheels do get results in this business.

Before you install the computer, your other source of leverage is threatening to defer delivery if things are not on schedule. Why should you accept and pay for the computer if your programs are not written, your room is not ready, your supplies have not arrived, and therefore you can't use the darn thing? This will definitely get the vendor to do cartwheels, because he normally pays a penalty to the manufacturer if he defers or cancels the machine.

When problems come up, express your displeasure to the people responsible. Be firm but fair and do not get hysterical. Programmers sometimes assume that anyone who loses his temper is a crackpot, and they may not take you as seriously as they would if you are calm. Ask for results and follow through to be sure they have done what they have promised to do.

When Things Go Well

When they do the job, you are really very lucky. While you might justifiably think that perfection ought to be the norm, in this industry it is sometimes still the exception. If your vendor comes through for you and you are happy with your system, please help him stay in business. Good ones are too few and far between. Do be a reference and demo site. Do talk him up to your friends. And do say thanks.

What Do You Do Now?

It would be nice to think that you would all close this book and rush to start the process of selecting a computer. Unfortunately, the cautions you have been given and the work that has been described may deter you from action and lessen your enthusiasm. But perhaps this is as it should be. Selecting a computer is a significant undertaking, and you should be really committed before embarking on the course. On the other hand, please don't let realism dampen your enthusiasm too much. Computers are, after all, the most significant tool since the wheel. And, if you have read this far, you deserve to have one!

Good luck!

PART
FOUR

Appendixes

A

Glossary of Terms

Acoustic Coupler— A device which connects a CRT or a computer to an ordinary telephone to allow communication with a computer at another location.

APL— Stands for "a programming language" and is a specific language used for interactive terminals.

Application Program— A computer program which instructs the computer to perform a particular job for you. These programs *apply* the computer to your needs. Examples of business applications include: Accounts Receivable, Payroll, and General Ledger.

Assembler Language— An early programming language that was structurally close to machine language. It is difficult to learn and rarely used for application development.

Backup— The process of making a duplicate copy of data stored on a disk or tape for security.

BASIC— The programming language most frequently used for microcomputers. BASIC stands for beginner's all-purpose symbolic instruction code.

Batch Processing— A concept in which data is grouped in batches, input to the computer, and proofed or edited together. In the early days of computers, this was thought to be the safest way to ensure accuracy of input. A batch of checks were typed into the computer as a group. The computer totalled the amounts, and the operator compared the total to a manually prepared adding machine tape. If the totals matched, the data had been entered correctly.

Baud— A term used to measure the speed with which data is transmitted between computer devices. Common rates included 300 baud and 1200 baud. These refer to the number of bits per second. A 1200 baud transmission is sending 1200 bits per second or approximately 150 characters per second.

Binary— A numbering system in which each digit stands for a power of two. It is used by computers because each position in computer memory can be in one of two states electronically—on or off. In our decimal numbering system each position, or digit, may contain one of ten symbols (0–9). To represent a decimal digit electronically requires 4 binary positions, or bits.

Bit— The smallest unit of information which may be read and understood by a computer. The term bit comes from a contraction of the words binary digit. The computer stores information electronically or magnetically in bits which are either on or off. It takes 4 bits in combination to represent a decimal digit. It takes 8 bits to represent an alphabetic character.

Blow Up— Slang for a program which does not run because of errors.

Bomb— Slang for a program which fails.

Buffer— A temporary holding area for data. For example, a buffered CRT allows you to type data into a buffered area where it may be examined and changed before it is transmitted to the computer. This speeds up processing.

Bug— A bug is a slang term used for either hardware or software malfunctions. The term comes from an early computer misadventure in which an actual bug was found inside the computer, causing mysterious malfunctions.

Bus— The device inside the computer in which all of the wires or conductors are joined. These include power, information, and address conductors. It is called a bus because a map of all the connecting wires looks like a bus route.

Byte— Eight bits make up a byte which may be used to represent any one of 256 characters—an alphabetic character, any decimal digit, or any special character. Computer memory and mass storage are measured in bytes.

Central Processing Unit (CPU)— The heart or brain of a computer. It contains the arithmetic, logic, and control functions of the computer. All computers from micros to mainframes have a CPU. The differences are measured in speed, sophistication of the instruction set, and the ammount of main memory available.

Chip— A small, thin wafer, usually made of silicon, containing thousands of circuits. It is housed in an integrated circuit which protects it and allows it to be electronically connected to other components. The entire integrated circuit (IC) is sometimes called a chip.

COBOL— A programming language standing for common business oriented language and used on larger computers.

Code— A slang term used by programmers referring to a program. "His code was terrible," meaning his programming was sloppy.

Command— An instruction to the computer. Some CRTs (or VDTs) have special command keys which allow you to give the computer an instruction such as print by depressing one key.

Compiler— A huge program which translates a programmer's instructions into machine language. The programmer's original code is referred to as the source program. After translation, or compilation, this machine language version is called the object program. The object program is used for day to day execution of that particular job. If the program has to be modified, it is the source program which is changed and then recompiled into a new object program. Compilers exist for all programming languages except those which are interpreted. *See* interpreter.

Computer— A device which can be programmed to receive, process, store, and output both arithmetic and alphabetic information. Electronic games are not computers because they perform only limited functions and cannot be programmed to perform multiple, general purpose jobs.

Computer Vendor— An organization which sells computers and/or programs.

Console— The primary CRT connected to the computer from which the operator controls computer operations.

CPS— Stands for characters per second, the way in which the speed of dot-matrix and letter-quality printers is rated.

Crash— When a computer stops working because of some malfunction.

CRT— Stands for cathode ray tube. It is essentially a TV screen married to a keyboard which is used to input data to the computer.

Cursor— A character on the screen of the CRT which lets the operator know what data the computer is expecting.

Data— Any information the computer receives as input, computes, stores, or outputs.

Data Base— A collection of data records or information. Data base systems or programs are used to create a data file.

Data Processing— (Sometimes called electronic data processing) The processing of information by a computer, including input, calculations, storage, and output.

Debugging— Solving either hardware or software problems.

Default— During the process of entering (inputting) data into a computer, certain information can be set up as a default to speed up data entry. For example, if you live in California and are entering new customer names and addresses, the computer can default to California as the state. The operator can override this for another state.

Degrade— The slowing down of computer speed or response time due to the overloading of the computer.

Desktop Computers— Another term for microcomputer.

Direct Access— The ability of a computer to go directly to a data record on disk without having to read the entire file.

Disk— A platter that resembles a phonograph record used to store data and programs. Information is stored magnetically in concentric circles called tracks.

Diskette— A small, flexible or "floppy" disk about the size of a 45-RPM record. It stores from 250,000 to over 1 million characters. Smaller diskettes called minifloppies holding 80,000 characters are available on personal computers.

Disk Drive— The device which holds the disk and which records information from the computer on the disk.

Documentation— The literature normally provided with a computer program to assist you in using it.

Dot-Matrix Printer— An inexpensive printer available with small computers. Characters are formed by wires in a matrix which reach out and form the letter or number on the page.

Edit— Reviewing input to ensure accuracy.

Eight-Bit (8-bit)— A processor chip which acts on one byte (8-bits) of data at a time.

Exception Report— A computer report which lists only information meeting specified criteria and needing management attention. For example, an inventory exception report lists only items that must be reordered, not the entire inventory.

Execute— The operation of a program. To execute the invoice program is to run invoices on the computer.

Field— A logical hunk of information stored in a computer data record. In the customer record are such fields as name, address, and zip code.

File— A logical collection of similar data records, such as customer file or inventory file.

Firmware— Software stored by the manufacturer in the ROM of a computer. The user cannot change or erase it.

Floppy Disk— See diskette.

Flow Chart— A logical diagram used to plan a program before beginning programming.

FORTRAN— A programming language standing for formula translation, commonly used for mathematical or scientific applications.

Hard Copy— Printed copy of information or data.

Hardware— The computer and its devices.

Head Crash— The destruction of a disk by the read-write head crashing into it. Rarely happens on the newer computers.

Initialize— To prepare something for use—either a program or a disk.

Input— The entry of data into the computer.

Instruction Set— The array of functions which may be performed on a particular computer or within a programming language.

Integrated Circuit— *See* chip.

Interactive— The input of data on a CRT with assistance from the computer. For example, you enter a customer number and the computer responds with the customer name and address, letting you see that the customer number was entered accurately.

Interface— The electronic connection between two computer devices.

Interpreter— A large program which translates a programmer's instructions into machine language each time they are executed. BASIC is most commonly interpreted as opposed to compiled. (See compiler.)

I/O— A common abbreviation of input-output. I/O devices include CRTs, disks, and printers.

K— An abbreviation for 1,000, or kilo. Computer memory (or RAM) is usually measured in Ks but each K is actually 1024. A 64K computer has 65,536 positions of main memory.

Keyboard— The portion of a CRT on which data is input. It resembles a typewriter married to a ten key.

Language— A means of communication with specific rules of grammar, spelling, and so on. Computer programming languages include BASIC, FORTRAN, and COBOL.

Letter Quality— The kind of printer producing fully-formed characters which look like they were typed. Used on computers that do extensive Word Processing.

Line Printers— A high-speed printer that produces an entire line of print at once (as opposed to character printers, which print one letter or number at a time).

Machine Language— The electronic binary instructions which the computer understands. Human programs are translated into machine language by compilers or interpreters.

Magnetic Tape— A tape containing data magnetically encoded which can be read by a computer. Data is written and read sequentially, whereas on a disk it may be read randomly.

Mainframe— The huge computers used primarily by Fortune 1000 companies.

Mass Storage— The devices which store your data inside the computer—usually disks or magnetic tape. Mass storage is not erased when the computer is turned off.

Mega— Abbreviation for 1 million. A 5 megabyte disk stores 5 million bytes, or characters.

Memory— (Sometimes called main memory.) The portion of the CPU which stores programs and data that are in actual operation. ROM and RAM are two types of CPU main memory. Memory size is usually measured in Ks.

Menu— A list of computer functions, usually displayed on a CRT, from which the operator selects the next program to run.

Micro— Small. A microcomputer is the smallest computer made.

Microcomputer— A small computer based on a microprocessor. Usually costs under $30,000.

Microprocessor— An integrated circuit that is extremely small and contains the essential ingredients of a CPU—arithmetic, logic, and control functions. It may also contain the CPU main memory. The advent of microprocessors has led to the dramatic proliferation of low-cost microcomputers.

Minicomputers— A small business computer which is more sophisticated in function than a microcomputer and which usually costs $40,000 to $100,000.

Modem— A contraction of two words, modulator and demodulator. A device which allows a computer to transmit and receive data over a telephone line.

Modulator— A device which may be attached to a personal computer allowing it to use an ordinary television set for output.

Monitor— Another term for a CRT, or television set, attached to a computer.

Multiprogramming— The simultaneous execution of more than one program by a computer.

Multiuser— A computer which may accommodate more than one simultaneous user. It may have multiple CRTs attached.

Networking— The connection of several computers which share data files.

Object Program— The machine language version of a program used when the computer performs that particular job. It is produced by a compiler from a source program.

Off-Line— Not directly connected to the computer. An I/O device may be taken off-line, or disconnected. Off-line data entry may be performed by keying information directly onto a diskette. This is then put on the computer to be read and processed.

On-Line— Connected to the computer. An on-line CRT immediately sends information to and receives information from the computer.

On-Site— At your location. On-site training or maintenance is performed at your office.

Operating System— The master program which resides in the main memory all the time and controls the operation of the computer.

Output— The information produced by the computer. It may be displayed on a CRT or a printer, or written on a disk.

Parallel— A term referring to the simultaneous operation of two functions. A parallel conversion is one in which functions performed on the computer are also continued in parallel under the old system until it can be verified that the programs work properly.

PASCAL— A relatively new, powerful language which can be learned and used modularly. Popular with students.

Password— A secret word which you type on the CRT allowing you to use the computer. It protects your programs and data from unauthorized users.

Peripheral Devices— Another term for I/O devices such as CRTs, disks, or printers. They are peripheral to the CPU.

Personal Computer— The smallest microcomputers made, affordable, but containing the essential functions of any general purpose computer.

PL/1— A very powerful programming language developed by IBM and not yet in general use on small computers. Stands for programming language #1.

Port— The portion of a CPU through which an I/O device may be connected. Computers have a fixed number of ports which indicate the maximum number of CRTs, disks, and printers which may be attached.

Printer— The primary output device of any computer, producing printed reports or hard copy.

Program— The instructions which cause the computer to perform a specific function in a precise way.

Programmer— A person who writes programs.

Prompt— A word or phrase displayed by a computer program on a CRT which asks the operator to enter specific information. For example, the operator is prompted to type in customer name by the prompt "NAME".

Punched Card— The original input medium used by computers. Data was stored on punched cards in the form of holes.

RAM— Stands for random access memory. The programmable, main memory used by the CPU for data and instructions. Its size is measured in Ks. RAM is erased each time computer power is turned off and changed every time you run a new program.

Random Access— Same as direct access.

Ranking Reports— A report produced in a meaningful sequence as a result of a computer sort. Customer records may be sorted by year-to-date sales, and a ranking report may be printed in this sequence.

Read-Write Head— The device inside a disk drive which reads and writes on a disk.

Record— A logical unit of information pertaining to a unique entity. A customer record contains all of the pertinent information about that one customer.

Response Time— The amount of time between entering data on a CRT and receiving an answer back from the CPU.

ROM— Read only memory. The portion of main memory which is preprogrammed by the computer manufacturer to perform certain functions. You cannot change or erase this information. On microcomputers, the operating system or the BASIC language interpreter may be stored in ROM.

RPG— A programming language standing for report program generator used on many minicomputers for business applications.

Save— A command which causes the computer to store or save certain instructions or data you wish to use again.

Screen— The television screen or display used by a CRT.

Scroll— The movement of data up or down on a screen, usually one line at a time.

Shared Logic System— A Word Processing system which has more than one CRT in simultaneous operation. Computers which have more than one CRT are called multiuser.

Sixteen-Bit (16-bit)— A processor chip which acts on 2 bytes (16 bits) of data at a time.

Software— Another term for one or more programs.

Sort— The automatic resequencing of data records on a disk. The customer records may be sorted (or arranged) alphabetically.

Source Program— The original program or instructions created by a programmer. It is written in an English-like programming language such as COBOL and is unintelligible to the computer until it is translated into machine language (or compiled into an object program).

Super-Minicomputers— Larger, more sophisticated minicomputers, usually costing over $100,000 and as much as $1 million.

Terminal— Another term for a CRT, VDT, and so on. An I/O device attached to a computer.

Throughput— The amount of information a computer can process in a specified period of time, the measurement of computer capability.

Timesharing— The shared use of a computer by multiple people, usually over a telephone line.

VDT— Stands for video display terminal. Another term for a CRT.

Winchester Disk— A hard disk stored permanently inside a computer.

Word Processing— A computer program which allows the entry and manipulation of text. Documents are stored on disk and may be efficiently changed and rearranged before printing.

B

Application Function Checklist

APPLICATION FUNCTION CHECKLIST
Order Processing Functions

Requirement		Application Function:	Vendor Response	
Necessary	Desirable	Order Processing Functions	Available Standard Package	Extra Charge
		Processing Steps:		
		Enter new orders		
		Order modification or cancellation		
		Order inquiry		
		Print picking slips		
		Enter actual shipped quantities		
		Print invoice		
		Automatic back order handling*		
		General Functions:		
		Post information to:		
		Accounts Receivable		
		Inventory Control		
		Sales Analysis		
		General Ledger*		
		Supports multiple companies*		

*Asterisks denote items probably not available if you are buying a microcomputer.

APPLICATION FUNCTION CHECKLIST
Order Processing Functions (*continued*)

Requirement		Application Function:	Vendor Response	
Necessary	**Desirable**		**Available Standard Package**	**Extra Charge**
		Supports multiple warehouses*		
		Credit memos reverse all entries*		
		Order Entry Functions:		
		Order entry screen tailoring*		
		Customer credit check before entering order*		
		Credit hold of order*		
		Multiple ship to addresses*		
		Inventoried and noninventoried items on order*		
		Special charges added to order		
		Stock available displayed with each line item entered*		
		Due date entered by line item		
		Substitute items suggested if stock unavailable*		
		Entry of comments with order*		
		Display of complimentary items*		
		Pricing, Billing, Discounting Functions:		
		Operator entered price		
		Automatic pricing:		
		Unique price for each item		
		Pricing by customer class		
		Quantity break pricing		
		Unity of measure conversions*		
		Assortable combinations*		
		Kit pricing*		
		Cost plus markup percentage*		
		List less discount by customer type		
		Chain discounting*		
		Contract pricing*		
		Minimum order surcharge*		
		Multiple taxing authorities		

*Asterisks denote items probably not available if you are buying a microcomputer.

APPLICATION FUNCTION CHECKLIST
Order Processing Functions (*continued*)

Requirement		Application Function:	Vendor Response	
Necessary	Desirable		Available Standard Package	Extra Charge
		Back Order Functions:		
		Automatic fulfillment upon receipt of inventory*		
		Promise date priority*		
		Even distribution across all back orders*		
		Priority given to selected customers*		
		Back orders maintained and listed: operator manually releases them		
		Order Processing Reports:		
		Order acknowledgments		
		Picking list		
		Picking list sorted by warehouse location*		
		Invoice		
		Invoice customized for you*		
		Bill of Lading*		
		Credit memo		
		Open order listing by order number		
		Open order listing by customer*		
		Open order listing by item*		
		New order listing by order number		
		New order listing by customer*		
		New order listing by item*		
		Back order listing by item*		
		Back order listing by customer*		
		Back order/stock receipt match by item*		
		Back order/stock receipt match by customer*		
		Credit memo register		
		Contract listing by contract number*		

*Asterisks denote items probably not available if you are buying a microcomputer.

APPLICATION FUNCTION CHECKLIST
Order Processing Functions (*continued*)

Requirement		Application Function:	Vendor Response	
			Available Standard	
Necessary	Desirable		Package	Extra Charge
		Contract listing by expiration date*		
		Invoice register		
		Daily sales journal		
		Sales rep commission report*		
		Backlog dollars by month*		
		Inquiry Screens:		
		Open order inquiry by order number		
		Open order inquiry by customer		
		Open order inquiry by item*		
		Back order inquiry by order number		
		Back order inquiry by customer*		
		Back order inquiry by item*		
		Daily sales tally*		
		Other:		

*Asterisks denote items probably not available if you are buying a microcomputer.

APPLICATION FUNCTION CHECKLIST
Accounts Receivable Functions

Requirement		Application Function:	Vendor Response	
Necessary	Desirable	Accounts Receivable Functions	Available Standard Package	Extra Charge
		Processing Steps:		
		Manual entry of invoice information		
		Automatic posting of invoice total from Order Processing		
		Entry of cash and checks received		
		Daily cash reporting and controls		
		Month-end reporting		
		Exception reporting		
		Inquiry handling		
		General Functions:		
		Balance Forward Accounts Receivable		
		Open item Accounts Receivable (cash is applied to specific invoices)		
		Multiple companies supported*		
		Alpha search technique used to identify customers (this allows you to use customer names instead of numbers).*		
		Variable aging periods*		
		Future aging*		
		Calculation of finance charges		
		Cash Receipts Entry:		
		Post cash against balance due		
		Post cash against a specific invoice		
		Post a partial payment		
		Pay on account*		
		Automatic application of check to oldest invoice*		
		Write-off capability*		
		Discount accounting*		
		Miscellaneous cash posting*		

*Asterisks denote items probably not available if you are buying a microcomputer.

APPLICATION FUNCTION CHECKLIST
Accounts Receivable Functions *(continued)*

Requirement		Application Function: Accounts Receivable Functions	Vendor Response	
Necessary	Desirable		Available Standard Package	Extra Charge
		Customer Information:		
		Name, number, address		
		Route		
		Telephone number		
		Contact name		
		Resale number		
		Credit limit		
		Terms		
		Customer sales class		
		Customer pricing class		
		Contract number		
		Salesman		
		Date of first sale		
		Date of last sale		
		Numbers of orders year-to-date		
		Sales month-to-date		
		Sales year-to-date		
		Profit month-to-date		
		Profit year-to-date		
		Profit percent year-to-date		
		Average number of days to pay		
		Amount due		
		Current due		
		Over 30 due		
		Over 60 due		
		Over 90 due		
		Over 120 due		
		Accounts Receivable Reports:		
		Invoice register		
		Cash receipts register		
		Statements		
		Statements for selected customers only*		
		Statements with payment tear strips*		
		Statements sorted by zip code*		
		Delinquency notices*		

*Asterisks denote items probably not available if you are buying a microcomputer.

APPLICATION FUNCTION CHECKLIST
Accounts Receivable Functions *(continued)*

Requirement		Application Function:	Vendor Response	
Necessary	Desirable	Accounts Receivable Functions	Available Standard Package	Extra Charge
		Aged trial balance		
		Accounts Receivable management and ranking reports:		
		Customers over credit limit*		
		Customers with delinquent balances*		
		Customers owing over a specified amount*		
		Invoices unpaid for over a specified number of days*		
		Customer aging reports by sales representative*		
		Mailing labels		
		Inquiries:		
		Customer receivables snapshot (Total and aged amounts due)		
		Customer open-item inquiry (Display of all unpaid invoices)		
		Total companywide Accounts Receivable snapshot (total you are owed)		
		Other:		

*Asterisks denote items probably not available if you are buying a microcomputer.

APPLICATION FUNCTION CHECKLIST
Inventory Management Functions

Requirement			Vendor Response	
		Application Function: **Inventory Management**	**Available** **Standard**	
Necessary	**Desirable**	**Functions**	**Package**	**Extra Charge**
		General Functions:		
		Item sales posted automatically from billing		
		Receipts, adjustments, and miscellaneous issues entered		
		Stock status reporting		
		Inventory valuation reporting		
		Inventory management/ exception reporting		
		Stock inquiries		
		Physical inventory/ subsystem*		
		Purchase order management subsystem*		
		Supports multiple warehouses*		
		Accounting Functions:		
		Multiple prices:		
		Quantity price breaks*		
		Customer class prices		
		List less discounts*		
		Multiple Costing Techniques:		
		Standard		
		Average		
		Weighted average*		
		Last cost		
		Landed cost*		
		Replacement cost*		
		LIFO or FIFO accounting*		
		Cost automatically updated when receipts are entered*		
		Stocking unit of measure different from pricing or costing unit of measure*		
		Shipping unit of measure different from stocking unit of measure*		
		Lot tracking*		
		Serial number trace*		
		Maintains inventory stock figures:		

*Asterisks denote items probably not available if you are buying a microcomputer.

APPLICATION FUNCTION CHECKLIST
Inventory Management Functions *(continued)*

Requirement		Application Function: Inventory Management Functions	Vendor Response	
Necessary	Desirable		Available Standard Package	Extra Charge
		Quantity on hand		
		Quantity on order		
		Quantity allocated		
		Quantity back ordered		
		Quantity available		
		Maintains sales statistics:		
		Quantity ordered*		
		Quantity sold		
		Quantity shipped*		
		Quantity back ordered*		
		Quantity returned*		
		Number of stockouts*		
		Desired sales statistics are maintained for the following periods:		
		Year-to-date		
		Current month-to-date		
		Last 12 months*		
		Last 24 months*		
		Additional Information to be Stored:		
		Manufacturer's item number		
		Item color*		
		Item size*		
		Item style*		
		Item class		
		Unit of measure		
		Shipping weight*		
		Substitute item*		
		Vendor number (primary source)		
		Vendor number (secondary source)*		
		Primary vendor lead time*		
		Secondary vendor lead time*		
		Warehouse location*		
		Date of last count*		
		Date of last sale*		
		Date of last receipt*		

*Asterisks denote items probably not available if you are buying a microcomputer.

APPLICATION FUNCTION CHECKLIST
Inventory Management Functions *(continued)*

Requirement		Application Function: Inventory Management Functions	Vendor Response	
Necessary	Desirable		Available Standard Package	Extra Charge
		Date of last cost change*		
		Date of last price change*		
		Physical Inventory Subsystem:		
		Preparation of count sheets and tags*		
		Comparison of actual count with book figures*		
		Variance report*		
		Adjustment update*		
		Valuation report*		
		Purchase Order Subsystem:		
		Entry of purchase orders		
		Printing of purchase orders*		
		Open purchase order reports*		
		by PO number*		
		by vendor*		
		by part number*		
		by due date*		
		Reconciliation of receipts with POs*		
		Quantities*		
		Cost*		
		Updating inventory stock figures appropriately*		
		Quantity on hand*		
		Quantity on order*		
		Costing figures*		
		Vendor analysis reports*		
		Inventory Analysis Aids:		
		Number of turns by item*		
		Number of turns for product class*		
		Average monthly usage by item		
		Number of months supply on hand by item		
		Customer service level*		
		Economic order quantity*		

*Asterisks denote items probably not available if you are buying a microcomputer.

APPLICATION FUNCTION CHECKLIST
Inventory Management Functions *(continued)*

Requirement		Application Function: Inventory Management Functions	Vendor Response	
Necessary	Desirable		Available Standard Package	Extra Charge
		Reorder point*		
		ABC reports		
		Inventory Reports:		
		Stock status reports		
		By item		
		By item within product class		
		By item within warehouse*		
		By item within vendor		
		Exception reports		
		Buyer's report		
		By item within vendor*		
		By item within buyer*		
		By item within product class*		
		Inventory Sales Analysis:		
		Sales by item		
		Sales by product class		
		Sales by vendor*		
		Profit percent year-to-date*		
		Profit year-to-date		
		Sales year-to-date		
		Unit sales		
		Inventory Valuation Report:		
		Value of on-hand and on-order stock*		
		By product class*		
		By vendor*		
		By buyer*		
		All items*		
		ABC analysis*		
		By sales*		
		By cost*		
		By profit*		
		Inventory audit trails		
		Receipts register		
		Issues and adjustments register		
		On order register*		

*Asterisks denote items probably not available if you are buying a microcomputer.

APPLICATION FUNCTION CHECKLIST
Inventory Management Functions *(continued)*

Requirement		Application Function: Inventory Management Functions	Vendor Response	
Necessary	**Desirable**		**Available Standard Package**	**Extra Charge**
		Warehouse transfer report*		
		Physical count variance report*		
		Physical count adjustmen· register*		
		Exception reports:		
		Overstock report		
		Reorder report		
		Expedite report*		
		Overdue stock report*		
		Others:		

*Asterisks denote items probably not available if you are buying a microcomputer.

APPLICATION FUNCTION CHECKLIST
Sales Analysis Functions *(continued)*

| Requirement | | Application Function: | Vendor Response | |
Necessary	Desirable	Sales Analysis Functions	Available Standard Package	Extra Charge
		Sales History		
		Month-to-date		
		Quarter-to-date		
		Year-to-date		
		Last 12 months*		
		Last 24 months*		
		Basic Sales Reports:		
		Sales by item		
		Sales by customer		
		Sales by sales rep		
		Sales by product class		
		Reports list:		
		Unit sales		
		Dollar sales		
		Profit		
		Reports may be ranked by sales or profit*		
		Detailed Sales Analysis:		
		Sales by item within customer*		
		Sales by item within sales rep*		
		Comparative Sales Analysis:		
		Sales or profit this year versus last for:		
		Items*		
		Product classes*		
		Customers*		
		Sales reps*		
		Product class within customer*		
		Product class within sales rep*		
		Item within customer*		
		Item within product class*		
		Graphs:		
		Sales by item*		
		Sales by customer*		
		Sales by product class*		

*Asterisks denote items probably not available if you are buying a microcomputer.

APPLICATION FUNCTION CHECKLIST
Sales Analysis Functions *(continued)*

Requirement			Vendor Response	
Necessary	**Desirable**	**Application Function:** **Sales Analysis Functions**	**Available Standard Package**	**Extra Charge**
		Graph to be displayed*		
		Graph to be printed*		
		Commission Accounting:		
		Computation of sales rep commission based on:		
		Line item sales*		
		Line item margin*		
		Invoice profit*		
		Accelerating scale*		
		Monthly commission report by rep*		
		Posting commission to payroll system*		
		Other:		

*Asterisks denote items probably not available if you are buying a microcomputer.

APPLICATION FUNCTION CHECKLIST
Accounts Payable Functions

Requirement		Application Function: Accounts Payable Functions	Vendor Response	
Necessary	Desirable		Available Standard Package	Extra Charge
		General Functions:		
		Distribution of expenses to appropriate General Ledger Account:		
		Builds and maintains Vendor Master File		
		Allows for entry of vendor invoices		
		Maintains open payables information		
		Maintains invoice due dates and lists items to be paid		
		Monitors discount due dates		
		Monitors recurring expenses to be sure they are automatically paid*		
		Prints cash requirements journal		
		Prints checks		
		Prints check register		
		Allows you to select invoices not to be paid, and automatically pays all others due*		
		Requires that you specifically flag each invoice to be paid		
		Allows for partial payments*		
		Allows for handwritten checks and after the fact entry of expense distribution*		
		Provides for bank check reconciliation*		
		Ages unpaid invoices for cash flow planning*		
		Allows you to select the aging periods*		
		Accounts Payable Reports:		
		Accounts Payable input listing		
		Invoice register		

*Asterisks denote items probably not available if you are buying a microcomputer.

APPLICATION FUNCTION CHECKLIST
Accounts Payable Functions *(continued)*

Requirement			Vendor Response	
Necessary	Desirable	Application Function: Accounts Payable Functions	Available Standard Package	Extra Charge
		Cash requirements report by vendor		
		Cash requirements report by due date*		
		Payment worksheet (invoices due to be paid)		
		Preliminary payment journal (invoices you have selected to pay)		
		Checks		
		Customized checks (your format)*		
		Check register (list of checks just written)		
		Expense distribution report		
		Aged payables report*		
		Vendor listing		
		Vendor analysis report (payments by vendor, year-to-date)*		
		Inquiries:		
		Vendor Master Inquiry		
		Open Payable Inquiry (look at all open invoices for a vendor)*		
		Companywide Accounts Payable snapshot (total amount you owe aged)*		
		Other:		

*Asterisks denote items probably not available if you are buying a microcomputer.

APPLICATION FUNCTION CHECKLIST
General Ledger Functions

Requirement			Vendor Response	
Necessary	Desirable	Application Function: General Ledger Functions	Available Standard Package	Extra Charge
		General Functions:		
		Allows you to build your Charts of Accounts		
		Automatically collects information from		
		Accounts Payable		
		Accounts Receivable*		
		Inventory Control*		
		Payroll*		
		Accepts manually entered journal entries		
		Allows for automatically recurring journal entries*		
		After monthly closing, produces		
		Income statements		
		Balance sheet		
		Provides for on-demand financial snapshot inquiries*		
		Allows for either 12 or 13 period fiscal year		
		Supports multiple companies*		
		Prints comparative information on financial statements		
		Actual versus budget		
		This year versus last*		
		Prints General Journal		
		Prints Recurring Journal*		
		Allows instant review of entries posted*		
		Provides year-to-date detail reports by account*		
		General Ledger Reports:		
		Chart of Accounts listing		
		General Journal		
		Recurring Journal*		
		Accounts Payable input listing		
		Payroll input listing*		
		Accounts Receivable input listing*		

*Asterisks denote items probably not available if you are buying a microcomputer.

APPLICATION FUNCTION CHECKLIST
General Ledger Functions *(continued)*

Requirement		Application Function:	Vendor Response	
Necessary	Desirable	General Ledger Functions	Available Standard Package	Extra Charge
		Income statements		
		Balance sheet		
		Comparative statements (budget to actual)		
		Comparative statements (actual this year versus last year)*		
		Year-to-date reports by account*		
		Financial reports on demand (without closing first)*		
		Financial Net Change Report*		
		Sources and uses of funds*		
		Allows you to customize the format of your reports		
		Inquiries:		
		Financial snapshot*		
		Status of an account*		
		Other:		

*Asterisks denote items probably not available if you are buying a microcomputer.

APPLICATION FUNCTION CHECKLIST
Mailing List Functions

Requirement		Application Function: Mailing List Functions	Vendor Response	
Necessary	Desirable		Available Standard Package	Extra Charge
		General Functions:		
		Allows you to build and maintain a mailing list file		
		Allows you to selectively mail to groups or individuals, based on:		
		Zip code		
		Customer or prospect classification		
		Business type		
		Sales representative		
		Product classification		
		Date of last mailing		
		Date of last contact		
		Date of last sale		
		Volume of sales, year-to-date		
		Prior attendance in a seminar*		
		Other:		
		_____		
		_____		
		_____		
		Produces labels		
		Interacts with Word Processing or Text Editor to produce personalized letters*		
		Produces a list of labels printed		
		Updates master record with date of mailing*		
		Updates master record with specific piece that was mailed*		
		Tracks information regarding a series of mailings (knows which pieces have been sent to whom)*		

*Asterisks denote items probably not available if you are buying a microcomputer.

APPLICATION FUNCTION CHECKLIST
Mailing List Functions *(continued)*

Requirement		Application Function:	Vendor Response	
				Standard Package
Necessary	Desirable	Mailing List Functions	Available	Extra Charge
		Mailing List Reports:		
		Listing of entire mailing file		
		Listing of selected groups according to parameters specified above		
		Labels		
		Personalized letters		
		Automatic list of labels produced		
		Other:		

---

*Asterisks denote items probably not available if you are buying a microcomputer.

APPLICATION FUNCTION CHECKLIST
Query and Report Writer Functions

Requirement		Application Function: Query and Report Writer Functions	Vendor Response	
Necessary	**Desirable**		**Available Standard Package**	**Extra Charge**
		General Functions:		
		Allows you to create a special file		
		Allows you to design and produce special reports		
		Allows you to format an inquiry screen		
		Report and screen design allow you to:		
		Give the report a title		
		Specify the data fields to be printed		
		Select records to be printed		
		Specify the sequence in which records will be printed (sort the file)		
		Define certain calculations to be made*		
		Ask the computer to total certain information		
		Selection capabilities include:		
		Selecting records based on comparing two fields (such as credit limit less than balance due)		
		Selecting records based on comparing a field with a constant (such as balance due greater than $2,000)		
		Selecting according to multiple criteria		
		Sorting capabilities allow you to:		
		Rank the report according to any data field (such as an aging report ranked by over 90 amount due)		
		Rank on multiple fields (such as amount due within sales rep)		

*Asterisks denote items probably not available if you are buying a microcomputer.

APPLICATION FUNCTION CHECKLIST
Query and Report Writer Functions *(continued)*

Requirement		Application Function: Query and Report Writer Functions	Vendor Response	
Necessary	Desirable		Available Standard Package	Extra Charge
		Rank the report according to a field which is calculated (such as profit percentage, computed from sales and cost figures in the record)*		
•		Allows you access to more than one file on your computer*		
		Allows you access to more than one file in one report*		
		Allows you to save the specifications for reuse		
		Other:		

*Asterisks denote items probably not available if you are buying a microcomputer.

Index

199